easy

francesca stone
Founder of Fall For DIY

HOMEMADE POTTERY

Make Your Own Stylish Decor
Using Polymer and Air-Dry Clay

PAGE STREET
PUBLISHING CO.

DEDICATION

For Ollen

"Be wild; that is how to clear the river." —Clarissa Pinkola Estés

PAGE STREET
PUBLISHING CO.

First published in 2020 by
Page Street Publishing Co.
27 Congress Street, Suite 105
Salem, MA 01970
www.pagestreetpublishing.com

Distributed by Macmillan, sales in Canada by The Canadian Manda Group.

24   23   22   21   2   3   4   5

ISBN-13: 978-1-64567-150-3
ISBN-10: 1-64567-150-3

Library of Congress Control Number: 2019957315

Cover and book design by Laura Benton for Page Street Publishing Co.
Photography by Francesca Stone

Printed and bound in the United States

contents

INTRODUCTION

There's nothing more satisfying than creating something useful and beautiful with your own hands. For me, it's even better when you can do it all without leaving your own home. When I talk about working with clay, most people jump to the conclusion I mean kiln-fired clay. But I'm here to show you that home modeling clays are just as good for creating stunning pieces for your home.

In this book, I use air-dry clay and polymer clay—both can be used at home to create everyday practical and decorative items. Yes, kiln-fired clay can have amazing results, but that is a difficult and expensive hobby to learn. It's my belief that home modeling clays are just as special: They are affordable, and they're available in hobby stores and online. The techniques are just as creative, and the finishes are endless. Sometimes we need to be creative to get the best from them, but to me that just makes the process more exciting.

I started working with clay after finishing my degree in textile surface design. I was working with jewelry and that naturally led me into the incredible world of polymer clay. I've spent the last ten years sharing the process on my blog, and many of those first projects came from a desire to share my love of clay with the world. As my ideas became more ambitious, I also started to experiment with air-dry clays, which opened up a whole new love of working with the material. And it seems you love it too! Some of my most popular craft DIYs to date are my clay tutorials.

Clay is easily one of my favorite materials to work with. The freedom of the process and the sheer scope of creative uses just keep me coming back to clay time and time again. Clay modeling will always have that hold on me because there's always something new to learn: a new way of mixing materials or a new finish, a different mold or pattern placement. You're never limited with clay.

I work with air-dry clay and polymer clay, and each brings different properties and benefits to the pieces we create. Use traditional treatments or experiment with ideas that have never been done before. Stick to the rules or break them. Make mistakes, have happy accidents and learn something new each time you pick up a new project.

It's the endless possibilities that keep clay exciting for me. It's a way to let your imagination run wild and flex your creative muscles. Creating projects with clay can be slow and thoughtful. You can become immersed in the clay, focusing on the process and taking yourself away from the stresses of the world. But it's also a great craft if you don't have hours of spare time to dedicate to it. You can create something beautiful even if you only have small pockets of time available. Many projects in this book are achievable in just half an hour, making clay a great material to work with if you want to commit to crafting more but you already have a busy schedule.

I've created the projects in this book to highlight how versatile and expansive your clay creations can be. Clay can be used in every room of your home to decorate, improve productivity and add personal touches that are unique to you. As you create the pieces in this book, you'll learn techniques for adding color, texture and pattern to your clay. You'll gain the skills and knowledge to build shapes and create containers, hooks and handles, holders and platters. As you build shapes and put these techniques together, you'll have the foundation to craft your own ideas and fill your home with beautiful clay creations.

Francesca Joy Stone

getting
started

All of the projects in this book can be created at home with simple, accessible materials and tools. Every project is achievable with little or no experience. Some of the projects are quicker than others. Some might need you to come back to them several times after waiting for the clay to dry and/or set before completing the final steps. The techniques I use are easy for beginners—although some, such as blending and joining, require more time and patience. It's best to tackle those projects when you have more time to dedicate to them.

There are many different clay brands you can use for these projects. My personal favorites are DAS and FIMO for air-dry clay. DAS clays are soft, and the terra-cotta is a beautiful shade. FIMO has a larger range of colors and they also come in smaller sizes for smaller projects. I also use FIMO polymer clay. I find it softer to use out of the packet than other brands, which means less time working and conditioning the clay before getting started.

Other polymer clay brands include Sculpey and Cernit. I've used both of these brands in the past and there's little difference. Some are easier to work with, but the outcome is the same quality. There are also non-branded clays available, which I wouldn't recommend using. These are less likely to have consistent colors, and the quality of your piece may suffer. FIMO, Sculpey and Cernit have large color selections, making it easy to find a similar color for the projects in this book no matter which brand you use.

There are many air-dry clay brands, and there isn't a "best brand" I can recommend. Each brand has slightly different properties. Some are firmer and some require more water to work with. Use the one you like best and can find easily. If you can, experiment with different brands and find one that suits your style of making!

It's important to get the right clay for your project, and it's also a good idea to invest in quality tools and materials if you can afford to. In my experience, lower-end tools sometimes break in my hand as I'm using them! Making one-time, carefully considered purchases will save you from buying the same items again and again. The same advice holds for items such as glue or varnish. A good glue creates a more stable bond, making your pieces last through more everyday wear and tear. Your varnish will provide protection from the environment. Investing in these items will prolong the life of your pieces.

Begin by reading through the Tools and Techniques section below. This will give you a solid understanding of how the clays respond and react to different techniques. You can only fully understand this through experience, so don't be afraid to pick up the clay and start experimenting. And be sure to read Getting the Most from the Clay (page 13). If you take care of your clay, you will be able to reuse it over and over until your piece is finished.

TOOLS AND TECHNIQUES

The best tools for creating with clay are your own hands! I really mean it. Feel the clay in your hands. Really dig in and don't be afraid to get them dirty.

Your hands can do a lot when you work with clay, but they can't do everything. Basic clay tools are affordable and easy to find. You can buy sets that include wire tools, wood blending tools, cutting tools and may also have scraping and smoothing tools. Buying a set gives you options and they're much more affordable than buying items individually. I find these bundles often include a few tools I won't use for years and then one day a project comes along that they are perfect for.

There are also plenty of useful items around your home that you can use to work the clay.

- Popsicle sticks make great smoothing and blending tools.

- Plastic or eco-friendly cornstarch straws are perfect for creating holes, as are toothpicks and skewers.

- Old makeup sponges make great blenders.

- A nail brush is the perfect texture for scoring clay before you join pieces.

- Buttons, fabric, glassware, yarn, plastic bottles, and even leaves and vegetables can add texture, make imprints and create patterns.

Get creative and experiment with the clay. What's the worst that can happen? Just roll up the clay and start again!

A selection of tools to use when working with clay.

Rolling out the clay.

rolling

Around 90 percent of my projects use a square wood dowel. These rolling support strips are one of the most important tools I use when I'm creating with clay. I use strips on either side of the clay as I roll it out. The roller runs over the clay and the strips to create an even thickness throughout the clay that we can easily measure and control. Starting every project with a quality base helps elevate the final result. Even if we go on to carve, bend and reshape the project, the base will stay strong and supportive.

Use scrap wood or ask for offcuts at a lumber or building supply store. Buying strips of wood is inexpensive, and you can even layer pieces together to get the right thickness. If you do choose to layer them, wrap both ends in masking tape. This will prevent them from slipping apart as you're working with them.

When it comes to rolling out the clay, I like to use an acrylic roller for its smooth, nonstick surface. Specialty clay rollers are best as they are stronger than those used in baking, but I also have a longer, acrylic kitchen roller for the times when I need the additional length. I do sometimes use a more traditional wood roller, usually when the clay is harder and I need a larger surface area to roll with.

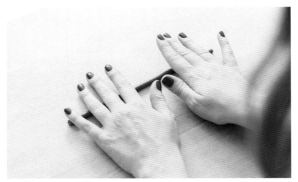

Rolling a tube shape from clay.

Always make sure the roller is clean and free of any residue from your last project. Then prepare the clay. If I'm using air-dry clay, I start by cutting off the amount I need. I place the piece facedown on its largest side on my nonstick surface between two lengths of wood. If I'm reusing a piece of clay, I add a little spray of water and roll it into a ball. I place the ball in position between the lengths of wood. I then press down to create a flat area on top of the ball, creating a surface to start rolling on.

Before I start rolling polymer clay, I always condition or work the clay until it is warm. Hold the clay between your palms to warm it. After 30 seconds, begin to manipulate the clay in your hands. Roll it out into a tube shape, twist it together and ball it back up several times until it is soft and pliable. Roll it back into a ball and place the ball between the wood, pressing down on the top with the palm of your hand. Start rolling over the flat area.

When you're rolling either type of clay, flip the clay over to ensure it is rolling evenly on both sides. You can also turn the clay 90 degrees to get a squarer piece. For some projects, especially planter making, you want longer pieces of clay. Don't rotate these pieces—you want the clay to stretch out as long as possible.

If you're using lengths of wood to help you roll the clay, keep pushing the roller back and forward over the entire piece of clay until it runs over both the clay and the wood at the same time. You will be left with a piece of clay that has an even thickness throughout.

I always use a large tile as my work surface. It is sturdy for rolling, nonstick and won't scratch or dent when I'm cutting the clay. Pastry and baking mats are easy to store away if you don't have a lot of space. These work just as well and often have handy cutting guides on them!

shaping

This book will show you a variety of achievable ways to shape and mold: Cutting simple designs by eye, using templates, making molds from household items, rolling, extruding, building up layers, using ready-made molds and working with your hands to push the clay into shape are just some of the techniques we explore.

This extensive range of techniques allows us to build the pieces without needing specialist skills. Instead, the projects use tools to create a shape that looks professional. These tools range from paper templates and kitchen utensils to specialized clay hobby tools. I've made sure all the tools are easy to find and inexpensive.

Shaping the clay with your fingers.

Cutting the clay.

Smoothing the clay.

Joining pieces of clay together.

cutting

I have two preferred ways of cutting. The first is using a length of wood or ruler as a guide and cutting with a sharp craft knife. The second is the trusty cookie cutter. A set of circle cutters is a worthwhile investment. I also have alphabet cutters, smaller shape cutters and specialty cutters for holidays and occasions. Fondant cutters are also a great way to shape thinner sheets of clay. In the Cookie Cutter Fridge Magnets project (page 156), I use them to create floral slabs.

This is not an exhaustive list of cutting techniques, and I use many more throughout these projects. A clay slicer tool is great for cutting thicker slabs of clay in one clean line, and a retractable/snap knife is something I always have in my toolbox.

Wire clay carving tools are essential for making more decorative cuts and shapes. These are used for carving clay from the piece rather than cutting the piece into a shape. We use these to make the grooves in the Pampas Vase (page 24).

smoothing

While we can always sand a piece smooth after it's dry or baked, it's advisable to smooth over the surface of the clay as best we can before setting. Polymer clay naturally has a smooth surface and will roll out flawlessly. When it does need some extra work around joins, warm the clay with your fingers first. When it's ready, you will find it easier to smooth over into a more even surface texture.

Air-dry clay is almost the exact opposite. It takes much more work to create a smooth surface in this softer, water-based clay. I keep a spray bottle of water on hand to keep the clay moist when I'm working with it and to help me smooth out the surface throughout the creative process. I use a range of tools for smoothing, including my own hands. I also use blending tools, sponges and wood scrapers to help achieve a smooth finish.

joining

Blending the clay together is an important skill to learn and, to be quite honest with you, it's a relatively simple one. You just need patience and a few tricks up your sleeve to create a smooth join that is difficult to spot once you've finished.

Polymer clay is much easier to join than air-dry clay. Its sticky texture creates a bond between two pieces of clay without needing to score or add more materials. The clay becomes malleable when warm: Working in a warm environment will give you an easier surface texture to work with. Alternatively, warm the area you need to join between your fingers or hands before beginning to blend. To blend the clay, apply a little pressure with your tool or your fingers. Smooth the clay from one side of the join over to the other. Keep moving the clay along the join until the line gets softer and disappears. Smooth out any bumps and imperfections from the clay you've moved until the surface is flat and even.

Air-drying clay.

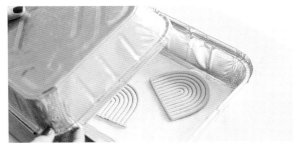

Baking polymer clay in the oven.

Air-dry clay needs more preparation before bringing the pieces together. Two smooth surfaces of clay will not create a strong bond and will break apart as they dry; we need to score or scratch the clay first. There are various tools you can use to do this, and any with a sharp or serrated edge will do the job. Score along the surface you want to join in opposite directions creating crosshatch grooves. Use your finger to add water to both pieces of clay and bring them together. Gently wiggle them into position to help create a bond. When you're happy with the positioning, blend the join using the same process as blending polymer clay and leave it to dry.

If you want to elevate your clay work, mix a little clay into your water to create a slip. This will help you to create a stronger join. When the water evaporates, the clay from the slip fills the gaps between the two pieces and strengthens the bond.

drying

As the name indicates, air-dry clay dries in the air. It is perfect for creating projects at home because you don't need any special equipment. Leave the clay to set on a piece of parchment paper on top of a flat, even surface in a warm, dry place. Any bumps in the surface will leave indents in the clay as it dries.

Turn the project regularly to allow for an even drying time on each side of the clay. When air-dry clay hardens, it also shrinks. We'll use this to our advantage, but we also have to be wary that this can create cracks, kinks and curving if we're not paying attention.

The clay will visibly change color as it dries. The outside will dry first, but the rest of the clay might not have hardened. Leave the clay for at least 24 to 48 hours depending on the thickness. Never use direct heat to dry your projects. Yes, you won't have to wait as long, but if the clay cracks you'll have to start again!

baking

Polymer clay needs to be baked in the oven to set. If you follow the instructions on the packet, it's perfectly safe to use your home oven to do this. An oven thermometer is a great investment for your polymer clay work. I swear by mine, and it's surprising how off-temperature ovens can be! If you keep checking it throughout the duration, the thermometer allows you to achieve and maintain the perfect temperature.

It's also useful to set a timer. Thankfully, my oven has a timer and switches itself off when the time is up—a setting that has saved the day more than once. I use my phone timer as a backup as well.

I always use two foil baking trays to bake my polymer clay. I place the clay in one tray, turn the other upside down and place it on top of the first to create a protective box. Foil trays come in a variety of sizes to suit any project. I use parchment paper or a ceramic tile placed in the tray. This helps to keep the clay flat and protected, and it also protects the foil. I haven't had to replace my trays yet!

cooling

I use the freezer to cool clay. This is a valuable tool to have at your disposal. It allows a temporary hardening of the clay, perfect for removing from molds, setting in shape and carving into the surface. When the clay warms again, the piece is as pliable as before. I often freeze the clay to check the shape is correct before baking it or leaving it to dry.

shaping

A hobby clay extruder is a great tool to invest in, but it's not essential. The extruder pushes clay through a small hole to create a long, consistent piece. The holes come in different shapes and sizes, such as circles, semicircles, squares, rectangular strips and droplets. In this book, I use the extruder to make a circular tube shape. You don't need an extruder to create this shape; you can roll out the clay by hand. This technique takes a little more time and skill. It will likely never be as "perfect," but sometimes the beauty of the work is in the imperfections.

FINISHING TECHNIQUES AND TREATMENTS

sanding

Sanding is such an integral part of the process, but it's one that is easy to overlook. It's tempting when you're excited about your creation to rush over this part. It took me years to learn the benefit of sanding; once I did, I never skipped this step again. Just 10 to 15 minutes of sanding can elevate the finish and give the piece a professional look.

Sanding removes cracks, bumps and imperfections in the surface of the clay. It also helps to remove small hairs and lint that are attracted to the sticky surface before the clay is cured. While it's sensible to take precautions to stop this from happening, it's often much easier to sand off a few imperfections than create something faultless in the first place.

We use two types of sandpaper when working with clay. When I want to sand air-dry clay, I use a medium-grain sandpaper—around 80 to 100 grit—for sanding out bumps. I use a fine-grain sand-

Sanding the dry clay.

paper—120 to 220 grit—for smoothing the surface. I always wear a dust mask when I'm sanding air-dry clay to protect myself from the clay particles.

When I want to sand polymer clay, I use wet-or-dry sandpaper. Again, a lower-grit sandpaper—around 240 grit—for more heavy-duty sanding. The higher numbers—around 1500 to 2000—will buff and shine the clay. Move your way from low to high to create a smooth surface texture.

varnishing

Neither air-dry clay nor polymer clay requires a finishing treatment, but there are many reasons you may want to use one. Air-dry clay will need protection from liquids. Water can damage and degrade the surface of the clay, and the clay will easily stain and absorb colors or oils. The best way to avoid this is to give the clay a protective layer. You might make the clay food-safe or add a glazed effect. Or you can use the varnish to decorate and accentuate the surface of the clay—it's not just about the practical applications.

There are types of varnish and gloss that have been specifically designed for this purpose. Polyurethane water-based varnish is popular, as it stays clear and will not yellow over time. Specialty polymer clay varnishes are available from clay suppliers. These all have varying properties and allow you to create different finishes. Some varnishes have a slight tint added that helps

Varnishing the clay.

Air-dry clay will create condensation on the inside of the bag. This is ideal, keeping the clay moist and ready to use. Polymer clay will stay dry; the clay is not water-based and will not mix with water. Polymer clay may harden over time. You can find softening products, such as liquid polymer clay or clay softener, at the same places where you buy the clay.

When using air-dry clay, I've found that coating my hands in a light, colorless oil, such as baby oil, helps to prevent the clay from sticking to my hands. This makes washing up easier and it helps to keep the clay smooth.

Have a spray bottle or a bowl of water on hand. Keeping the clay moist gives you longer to work with it and improves the surface texture, especially if you're blending.

Dust and hairs can get on the surface as you work with the clay. Work on a clean, dry surface, and make sure to use a microfiber cloth or cleaning wipes to help you avoid leftover fibers. Avoid wearing clothes that can shed fibers or are difficult to keep out of the way. Wool sweaters are one of the worst offenders. An apron is a great way to keep clay away from your clothes and to keep your clothes away from the clay as well! When working with air-dry clay, make sure your hands and any tools are clean and dry before adding oil or water.

you see where the varnish has been applied; it vanishes as the varnish dries. My favorite food-safe varnish is Decopatch Aquapro. Its finish is waterproof and washable, making it perfect for any kitchen project.

You can use other household substances that will act like a varnish, including watered-down PVA glue, nail varnish, spray varnish and wax. These all act differently on the surface, giving you a different finish. It's best to experiment on a tester piece of clay before using them.

Apply any varnish in light layers using a foam brush. Wait until each layer has dried fully before you apply the next coat. We do this to avoid cracking and pooling in the varnish. The instructions on each varnish will give you the drying times.

GETTING THE MOST FROM THE CLAY

Keeping your clay in good condition will save you time and save you money. When you've finished using your clay, whether it's air-dry or polymer clay, the best place to store it is in an airtight container. I keep ziplock bags with my clay supplies. Place the clay in the bag, push the excess air out of the bag and close the seal. This will preserve your clay for weeks, if not months.

If you do find any fibers in your clay, you can use clear adhesive tape to remove them. Lightly tap the sticky side over the surface of the clay to remove looser pieces. If that doesn't work, take a clean, flat blade, such as a clay slicer tool, and gently run it across the surface. Clean the blade each time you do this to prevent marking the clay. If you find you still have fibers in the clay, you can wait until it has set and sand off any remaining pieces.

living

Our living spaces are often the areas where we spend the most time at home. They are the heart of the home, a welcoming space that is comforting and relaxing. And they're also a place to inject some personality.

I love to add a lot of greenery to my spaces, so beautiful planters are always at the top of my making list. In this chapter, we have three planters and each one encompasses a variety of techniques and alternative ways to use the clay. In the Speckled Arch Planter (page 32), we even mix both air-dry and polymer clay together—something I never thought I'd do! It works perfectly and is a welcome reminder that sometimes we need to think outside the box.

This chapter includes many other useful decorative items. Creating a terrazzo-style surface design is a popular way of making your polymer clay pieces more interesting. I've used this technique to create wall hooks (page 20) that make the most of this classic design.

One of my favorite projects in this book is the Light-Up Layered Tealight Holder (page 37). It's a simple design and it's easy to make. Another easy but elegant project is the Tie the Knot Ornament (page 43), which explores a different way to shape clay. Using an extruder creates a perfectly uniform tube that we can twist, knot and bend into shape. Personally, I think this would make a great engagement gift for anyone, you know, tying the knot!

BUBBLE POP PLANTER

If you're anything like me, you have plants piled on window ledges and shelves around the house. These spaces are ideal for experimenting with color, shape and texture. Use planters to add accents that create interesting compositions all around your home.

This project is an example of combining simple techniques to make something with a big visual impact. The planter adds a spark of fun to any green spot, and it turns a simple pot into something visually striking. The bubbles can hide any irregularities, so it's a great way to practice your pot making. I think this style suits a more imperfect, handmade, quirky look, adding to the whimsical tone of the piece.

materials

5 oz (150 g) leaf green FIMO polymer clay

Roller

0.5 oz (15 g) white FIMO polymer clay

0.2 oz (5 g) black FIMO polymer clay

2 (1 x 15 x 0.25" [2.5 x 38 x 0.6–cm]) lengths of wood

2.5" (6-cm) circle cookie cutter

Parchment paper

2 (1 x 15 x 0.13" [2.5 x 38 x 0.3–cm]) lengths of wood

Ruler

Craft knife

Flat blending tool

2 (10 x 10" [25 x 25–cm]) foil baking trays

1. Start by mixing the clay together. Break the large green piece into four pieces and warm each one in the palms of your hands. Use the roller to roll it out as thin as you can. This might be difficult as you have not worked the clay soft yet; don't worry if you can't roll it out too thinly. Break the white and black clay into four roughly even pieces. Add one of each to your four green blocks. Warm each block between your palms once again. Start rolling it into a tube, then back into a ball several times until the clay feels soft and malleable and the colors are mixed together. When it is ready, add the next piece of clay and repeat the process until all the clay is in one ball and shows a solid color.

2. Place the soft clay on a nonstick surface. Place the 0.25-inch (0.6-cm)-thick lengths of wood on either side. Roll out the clay until the roller runs smoothly over the clay and it's an even thickness with the wood.

3. Press the cookie cutter into the surface of the clay, using the flat of your hand to apply even pressure. Twist the cutter slightly in both directions to prevent it from sticking to the clay. Lift the cutter out of the outer piece of clay. Gently press the circle of clay left inside the cutter out to one side on a piece of parchment paper.

4. Roll the leftover piece back into a ball and place it between the 0.13-inch (0.3-cm)-thick lengths of wood.

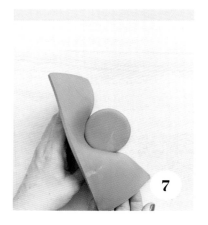

5. Roll out the clay until the roller runs smoothly over the clay and it's an even thickness with the wood.

6. Measure and cut an 8 x 3–inch (20 x 7.5–cm) rectangular piece of clay.

7. Wrap the longer edge around the circle piece of clay you cut out. Carefully line up the long edge with the bottom of the clay circle.

8. Bring the two shorter edges of the rectangle together so they meet along the 0.13-inch (0.3-cm) side. Push them together gently.

9. Warm the clay on both sides of the join with your fingers, then use a flat blending tool to blend the clay along the join on both the outside and inside. Place the pot to one side.

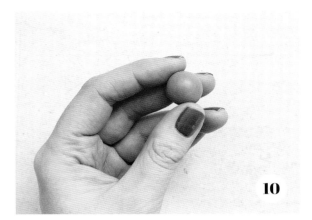

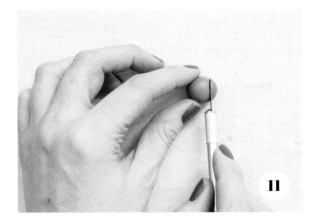

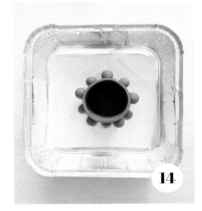

10. With the remaining clay, weigh out fourteen pieces that are 0.15 ounces (4 g) each. Roll each one into a ball, smoothing out any cracks or creases in the clay.

11. Use the craft knife to cut off a small piece from one side of the ball. Repeat with each ball, then weigh a piece from the offcuts. Roll this piece into one last ball and cut off the piece from the edge again.

12. You will now have fifteen balls of clay ready to attach to the pot. Score the flat edge of each ball by carving lines into the surface with the craft knife. Firmly press the first ball of clay to the pot about 0.5 inch (1 cm) from the top

edge. Place another four at this distance from the top at even intervals. Press five balls along the center of the pot, evenly spaced between each ball in the first row.

13. Place the last row of balls about 0.5 inch (1 cm) from the bottom of the pot vertically in line with the first row.

14. Preheat the oven to 230°F (110°C). Line a foil baking tray with an 8 x 8-inch (20 x 20-cm) piece of parchment paper. Carefully transfer the pot to the foil tray and cover it with a second tray. Heat it in the oven for 30 minutes. When the time is up, remove the tray from the oven and leave the clay to cool entirely before lifting the clay out.

HUNG UP ON TERRAZZO WALL HOOKS

Wall hooks are one of the most underused items in most homes. Hear me out. They are useful in every setting. So much clutter can be put into fabric or string bags and hung up in seconds: fruit, toys, beauty products and silk scarves, to name just a few. Hooks are also great for tidying up coats, hats, scarves, shopping bags, blankets, aprons, hanging planters, artwork and pendant lighting. I could go on, but you get the idea. Creating curated areas featuring wall hooks can look amazing, and they save you time and energy in the daily fight against clutter.

These terrazzo hooks give a nod to the latest trend, but in a subtle, timeless way. The monotone color scheme fits easily into any decor, and it won't look outdated when the trend is over. This is a great project if you have a limited amount of clay: All you need is black and white, making this perfect for using up leftover clay from other projects.

materials

2 oz (57 g) white FIMO polymer clay

2 oz (57 g) black FIMO polymer clay

Roller

Craft knife

2 (1 x 15 x 0.25" [2.5 x 38 x 0.6–cm]) lengths of wood

1.25" (3-cm) circle cookie cutter

0.75" (2-cm) circle cookie cutter

Pointed sculpting tool

Double-ended dowel screws

8 x 8" (20 x 20–cm) tile

1 (10 x 10" [25 x 25–cm]) foil baking tray

Fine-grain wet-or-dry sandpaper

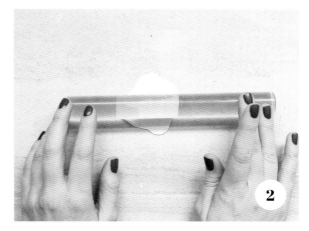

1. Take 0.35 ounces (10 g) of white clay from the block. Hold it between your palms for 30 seconds to warm it up. Roll it in your fingers until it is soft and smooth. Take a small pinch of black clay and work this into the white clay, rolling, twisting and balling up the clay until the color is consistent throughout.

2. Break off about one-quarter of the clay and roll it out thinly using just a roller.

3. Using a craft knife, cut the clay into small pieces. Run the knife through the clay in different directions so the pieces are randomly shaped. You want to make the pieces pea-sized or smaller.

4. Place these to one side. Repeat the process, adding a small pinch of black to the remaining white clay, breaking off another quarter and cutting it into pieces. Repeat this two times, until you have a range of hues cut into small, angular pieces of clay.

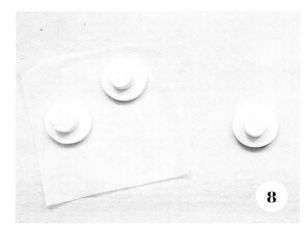

5. Take the remaining white clay out of the packet and work it between your hands until it is soft and warm. Place it on a nonstick surface between two 0.25-inch (0.6-cm)-thick lengths of wood. Roll it out until the roller runs smoothly over the clay and it's an even thickness with the wood.

6. Place the cut pieces of clay over the surface in a random pattern. Overlap some of the pieces to create the terrazzo look.

Keep the wood pieces in place and roll over the clay once again to create a smooth flat surface.

7. Press the larger cookie cutter into the surface of the clay. Give it a twist in both directions, then take it back out of the clay. Gently push the circle of clay from inside the cookie cutter and place it to one side. For each 1.25-inch (3-cm) circle, also cut two 0.75-inch (2-cm) circles.

8. To construct the wall hook, place one 0.75-inch (2-cm) circle on top of another. Blend these together around the join. Turn one 1.25-inch (3-cm) circle over so that the pattern is facing down. Place the two smaller circles into the center of the larger circle and use a pointed sculpting tool to blend the join.

9

9. Gently twist a dowel screw into the center of the smaller circles. Make sure not to push it all the way through all three circles. You can mark about 0.5 inch (1 cm) along the screw to make sure you don't push it in too far.

Preheat the oven to 230°F (110°C). Place the hooks facedown on a tile in a foil baking tray to bake in the oven. Make sure they are on a flat surface—any bumps underneath the hooks will imprint onto the surface of the clay. Heat the tray in the oven for 30 minutes. When the time is up, remove the tray from the oven and leave the clay to cool entirely before lifting it out. Be careful: The metal screws will be very hot. Don't touch these for 30 minutes or until they are completely cool.

Wet the surface of the clay and rub it with the sandpaper until the surface is smooth.

PAMPAS VASE

Dried grasses are having a major resurgence right now, just like pretty much anything that was popular in the 1970s. You can't go wrong using them in your home decor because they are such a fantastic way to add depth and texture. I like their longevity, especially because I struggle with houseplants and don't want the expense—or mess—of fresh flowers year-round.

Dried arrangements also give you more creative freedom when designing and making clay vases at home. This vase is not meant for water. Use dried and artificial flowers only, please. Even without any flora, this vase is a thing of beauty. Place it on a shelf among a curated collection of beautiful objects for a vignette that's always Insta-worthy.

materials

Ruler

Pencil

3" (7.5-cm)-diameter mailing tube

Craft knife

35 oz (1 kg) white DAS air-dry clay

2 (1 x 15 x 0.25" [2.5 x 38 x 0.6–cm]) lengths of wood

Roller

Damp sponge

Round metal carving tool

Parchment paper

Flat blending tool (optional)

3.5" (9-cm) circle cookie cutter

Medium-grain sandpaper

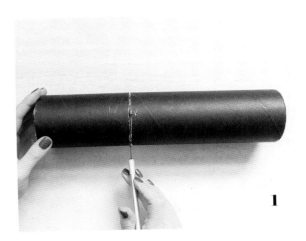

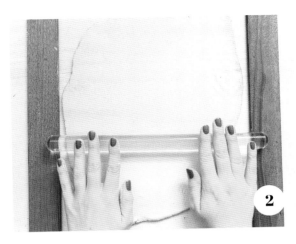

1. Measure and mark 8 inches (20 cm) from one end of the mailing tube. Using a craft knife, cut the tube into two pieces at that point. I find it helps to lightly score the line around the tube first to keep it straight.

2. Place your block of clay between the lengths of wood on a nonstick surface. Roll out the clay. Keep turning the clay every five to ten rolls to make sure you end up with a piece that is almost a square.

3. Measure and mark 9.5 x 8 inches (24 x 20 cm) in the piece of clay, ensuring all corners fit onto the piece of the clay you have rolled. Use a craft knife and the straight side of the wood to cut along each side.

4. Remove the excess clay. Using water and a sponge, smooth over the surface and edges of the rolled-out clay.

5. Gently score a line about 0.5 inch (1 cm) inside from the edge, along both of the 8-inch (20-cm) sides of clay. You'll need to smooth this line out later; the lighter you press, the easier it will be.

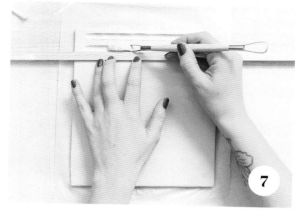

6. Place a piece of wood 0.75 inch (2 cm) from the edge of the longer side. Use this piece of wood as a guide when you cut the clay with the carving tool. Gently line up the end of the carving tool with your scored line in the clay. Press the tip into the clay while holding the tool at a 45-degree angle. Once the tool is submerged into the clay at its widest part, run it along the wood to the opposite side. Just before you reach the other end, take the tool out and place the tip of the second line holding the tool so it is at a 45-degree angle again—this time facing the opposite direction. Repeat the action of gently pressing the tool into the clay until it meets the groove you just made.

7. Remove the excess clay and move the wood down 0.75 inch (2 cm). Repeat the action with the carver tool to create another groove. Continue to make the grooves along the surface until you reach the other end of the clay.

8. Wet the sponge with a little water and smooth over the surface of the clay. Use your finger in each groove to smooth over any cracks or rough areas.

9. Carefully lift the clay onto a piece of parchment paper and fold the parchment paper over around an inch (2.5 cm) from one of the shorter ends. Lift this end onto the mailing tube. Pull back the parchment paper as you wrap the clay around the tube, holding it in place with your other hand.

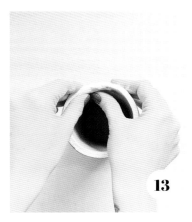

10. When the clay wraps around the entire tube, wet the edges where they meet and gently blend them together with your fingers or a flat blending tool.

11. Leave the clay to dry for 24 hours. It will be dry on the outside; if the clay still has darker patches, leave it to dry until the outside looks bright white. Very gently push the mailing tube out of the center. If the clay begins to move out of shape, stop and leave it to dry for another 24 hours.

12. Roll out the remaining clay between the lengths of wood. Cut a circle with the cookie cutter. Wet and score just inside the edge of one side of the circle. Place this on the bottom of the vase and blend the outer edge of the clay over the join to create a seamless join.

13. Take small pieces of clay, wet them and blend them to the inside of the vase along the join to hide the seam.

14. Leave it for 24 hours to dry, then sand it smooth using a medium-grain sandpaper.

BLOCK PARTY BEADED WALL HANGING

Using clay to make beads for use in jewelry is a tradition that goes back thousands of years. In this project, we're stripping this technique back to its bare bones and creating a pattern by placing the beads in blocks of color. The result is a piece of art made from clay beads that works perfectly in a modern picture wall.

Bead making is a therapeutic exercise. The repetitive nature makes it the perfect craft for a podcast or TV binge. Don't rush through the process, and take your time with each bead to create your spheres. Warming and cooling the clay is an integral part of this project. You'll need warm, soft clay to roll the beads and harder, cool clay to make the holes without pushing the beads out of shape.

materials

2 oz (57 g) white FIMO polymer clay

2 oz (57 g) chocolate FIMO polymer clay

2 oz (57 g) mustard FIMO polymer clay

2 oz (57 g) terra-cotta FIMO polymer clay

Craft knife

Ruler

2 (10 x 10" [25 x 25–cm]) foil baking trays

Toothpick

Parchment paper

Wood skewers

Scissors

Thin cotton cord

0.25" (5-mm) round wood dowel

Strong multipurpose glue

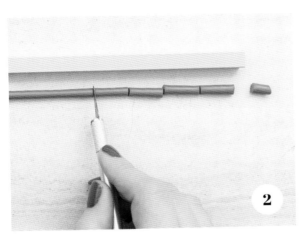

1. Remove the clay from the packet and break into four quarters. Hold each quarter between your palms to warm the clay. After 30 seconds, begin to work the clay in your hands. Roll it out, twist it together and ball it back up several times until it is soft and pliable.

2. Roll the clay out into a long tube. It should be around about 0.25 inch (5 mm) thick. Cut the tapered ends off the tube so that it is a consistent thickness throughout. Place this next to a ruler. Cut the tube into 0.75-inch (2-cm) sections using the craft knife to get a clean cut.

3. Individually warm up each 0.75-inch (2-cm) piece of clay by rolling it around your palms. Then, using your fingertips, roll the clay into a ball using a hard surface to gently roll the clay in circles.

Repeat with each piece of clay until your beads are even balls. Place them in a foil baking tray in the fridge to cool and temporarily harden.

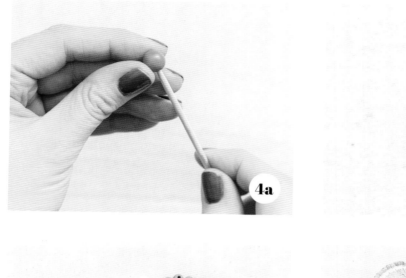

4a

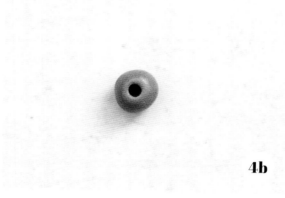

4b

5

6

4. Using a toothpick, make a hole in the bead by gently twisting the toothpick through the cooled clay (see image 4a). If the clay is too soft or you push too hard, the bead will squeeze out of shape. When the toothpick reaches the other side of the bead, twist it back out and go back through in the opposite direction. This will ensure the hole is smooth and uniform throughout (see image 4b).

5. Make 35 beads in white, 32 beads in chocolate, 39 beads in mustard and 38 beads in terra-cotta.

6. Preheat the oven to 230°F (110°C). Line a foil baking tray with an 8 x 8–inch (20 x 20–cm) piece of parchment paper. Slide the beads onto skewers and place into the foil tray, ensuring they are spaced and not touching as they set. Cover it with a second tray and bake for 30 minutes.

7. Cut fifteen 12-inch (30-cm) lengths of cord and tie them along the dowel. Thread the beads onto the cord to make a pattern in the following order from left to right:

9 white beads, 7 chocolate beads

8 white beads, 8 chocolate beads

7 white beads, 9 chocolate beads

6 white beads, 1 terra-cotta bead, 5 chocolate beads, 4 mustard beads

5 white beads, 2 terra-cotta beads, 3 chocolate beads, 6 mustard beads

8 terra-cotta beads, 8 mustard beads

9 terra-cotta beads, 7 mustard beads

9 terra-cotta beads, 7 mustard beads

9 terra-cotta beads, 7 mustard beads

8. Tie a knot at the end of each piece of cord just after the last bead. Add a dab of glue to the knot, and when it is dry cut off the excess cord.

9. Cut a piece of cord 20 inches (50 cm) long. Tie one end of the cord to one end of the dowel and the other end of the cord to the other end of the dowel.

SPECKLED ARCH PLANTER

Once you start making arches with clay, it's impossible to stop! Their symmetrical shape adds a pleasing visual element to any object, taking something that is quite simple and creating a statement piece. For this project, I also wanted to explore speckled clay. It creates a beautiful surface design easily and quickly, and it gives your clay that little extra oomph.

You'll create the white speckles for this look using air-dry clay. The dried clay will give you the perfect speckled look without the risk of it blending into the polymer clay. The dried air-dry clay is easy to grind into pieces and can cope with the temperatures used for heating the polymer clay. Use a small blender or an immersion blender to help grind the air-dry clay down to size. Just blitz the clay once or twice to create small enough pieces.

materials

0.35 oz (10 g) white DAS air-dry clay	2.75" (7-cm) circle cookie cutter
Roller	2 (1 x 15 x 0.13" [2.5 x 38 x 0.3–cm]) lengths of wood
Hair dryer (optional)	
Small blender or immersion blender (optional)	Ruler
	Flat blending tool
Craft knife	
9 oz (250 g) terra-cotta FIMO polymer clay	Clay extruder (optional)
2 (1 x 15 x 0.25" [2.5 x 38 x 0.6–cm]) lengths of wood	2 (10 x 10" [25 x 25–cm]) foil baking trays
	Parchment paper

1. A day before you want to make this planter, make the white flecks to accent the terra-cotta clay. Roll out the air-dry clay as thin as you can make it and leave it on a nonstick surface to dry. If you're in a rush, use a hair dryer to speed-dry the clay; we're not worried about cracking or damaging the clay.

2. Once the air-dry clay is completely dry, break it up into tiny pieces. I used a blender to speed this step up; I use a separate blender container for all my clay needs. I pulsed twice to get the right consistency. If you don't want to use a blender, break up the clay with your fingers and then use a craft knife to finely chop it. Put the pieces to one side and clear your work surface.

3. Cut the terra-cotta clay into four pieces and warm each one in your hands, rolling and balling up the clay until it is soft and easy to manipulate. When all the clay is soft, bring it back together into a ball.

4. Place the soft clay on a nonstick surface between the 0.25-inch (0.6-cm)-thick lengths of wood. Roll out the clay until the roller runs smoothly over the clay and it's an even thickness with the wood.

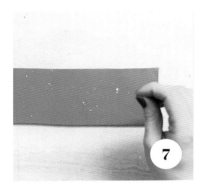

5. Press the cookie cutter into the surface of the clay, using the flat of your hand to apply even pressure. Twist the cutter slightly in both directions to prevent it from sticking to the clay. Lift the cutter out of the outer piece of clay. Gently press the circle of clay left inside the cutter out to one side on the nonstick surface.

6. Roll the leftover piece back into a ball and place it between the two 0.13-inch (0.3-cm)-thick lengths of wood. Roll out the clay until the roller runs smoothly over both the clay and the wood, creating an even thickness throughout the clay. Measure and cut a rectangular piece of clay that is 9 x 3.5 inches (23 x 9 cm).

7. Take a pinch of the ground-up air-dry clay and, holding your hand around 12 inches (30 cm) above the clay, slowly sprinkle the small pieces over the surface of the clay. When you're happy with the placement, lightly brush off any larger piles of clay with your fingers.

8. Gently run the roller over the clay, securing the white speckles in place.

9. Wrap the longer edge around the circle piece of clay. Carefully line up the long edge with the bottom of the clay circle. Bring the two shorter edges of the rectangle together so they meet along the 0.13-inch (0.3-cm) side. Push them together and gently warm the clay on both sides of the join with your fingers. Use a flat blending tool to blend the clay along the join on both the outside and inside. Place the pot to one side.

10. Take the remaining clay and roll, squeeze and stretch it repeatedly until it's soft and warm.

11. Cut off about a quarter of the clay and roll it into a rough tube shape about the same size as the extruder tube. Push this into the clay extruder. If you don't have an extruder, roll the clay into a thinner tube to create the arches. You'll need to take your time rolling sections to about 12 inches (30 cm) long at a time. Move your hands along the tube as you roll to keep the thickness even.

12. If you're using the extruder, insert the circle extruder part and push the clay out to make the thin tubes; follow the extruder instructions to do this. If your clay is warm and pliable, it should come out in a smooth tube. If the clay is cracked, remove it from the extruder and work it in your hands again as described in Step 3.

13. Take another pinch of your ground-up air-dry clay. From the same height as before, sprinkle it onto the nonstick surface. Gently roll the tube over the sprinkles once or twice without using any pressure. Remove the clay from the sprinkled clay; brush off and clear up any excess air-dry clay.

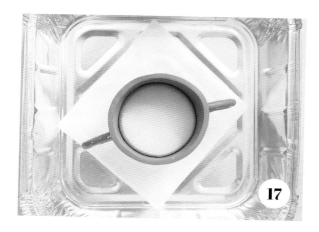

14. Once you have the tube ready, it's time to make the inner arc. Gently fold the clay onto itself around about 0.5 inch (1 cm) from one end, gently pressing the two sides together without distorting the shape. Cut off the longer length of clay where it meets the beginning.

15. Next, line up one end of the remaining clay tube with the beginning of this first arch. Run the tube over the arch to the other end, gently pressing it into place. Cut off the excess again in line with the straight edge of the arch.

16. Repeat the last step two more times to complete the arm of the planter. Make one more arm for the opposite side of the pot. Press the arms into the planter in a centered position. The clay will easily adhere with a little pressure. Hold one hand inside the planter while gently applying pressure with the other hand holding the arm in place.

17. Preheat the oven to 230°F (110°C). Line a foil baking tray with an 8 x 8–inch (20 x 20–cm) piece of parchment paper. Carefully transfer the pot to the foil tray. Cover it with a second tray and bake it in the oven for 30 minutes. When the time is up, remove the tray from the oven and leave the clay to cool entirely before lifting it out.

LIGHT-UP LAYERED TEALIGHT HOLDER

This tealight holder takes the simple technique of layering clay and turns it into a platform for a candle. Add it to a shelf for depth and character, or place it on a coffee table as a beautiful accent piece. You can create the design and have it ready to bake in just 15 minutes. The trick is to use wood strips to roll the clay and work on the parchment paper to ensure that removing and stacking your clay circles is easy.

When you're making a candleholder, always use polymer clay. Air-dry clay has an almost paper-like quality to it that will burn. It's much safer to use polymer clay. With any material around naked flames, please be vigilant. Never leave a flame unattended. Don't let the flame burn right down or touch the clay.

materials

3.5 oz (100 g) taupe FIMO polymer clay

2 (1 x 15 x 0.13" [2.5 x 38 x 0.3–cm]) lengths of wood

Roller

3.5" (9-cm) circle cookie cutter

2.5" (6-cm) circle cookie cutter

2" (5-cm) circle cookie cutter

1.5" (4-cm) circle cookie cutter

2 (10 x 10" [25 x 25–cm]) foil baking trays

Parchment paper

Fine-grain wet-or-dry sandpaper

Tealight

1. Break the clay into four quarters. Hold each quarter between your palms to warm the clay. After 30 seconds, begin to work the clay in your hands. Roll it out, twist it together and ball it back up several times until it is soft and pliable. Start working all the pieces of warm clay back together into a ball.

2. Place the clay on a nonstick surface between the lengths of wood. Roll out the clay until the roller runs smoothly over the clay and it's an even thickness with the wood. Using the cookie cutters, cut out three circles—one 3.5 inches (9 cm), one 2.5 inches (6 cm) and one 2 inches (5 cm). Press the cookie cutter into the clay and twist a little in both directions. Remove the cutter and circle of clay.

3. Place the 1.5-inch (4-cm) cookie cutter in the center of the 2.5-inch (6-cm) piece of clay. It's worth taking some time to find the correct placement in the middle of the outer circle, as this will help the candleholder look balanced. Press the cookie cutter into the clay and twist a little in both directions. Remove the cutter and circle of clay.

4. Place the outer ring you're left with onto the largest circle of clay. Gently press it into place with your fingertips. Avoid pressing the edges down; you want to keep them crisp.

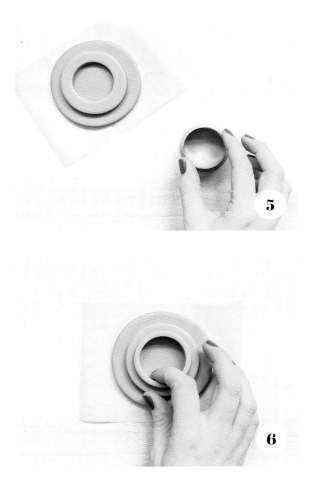

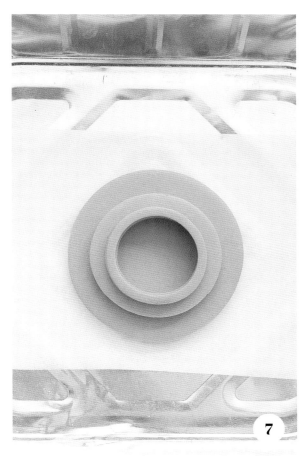

5. Place the 1.5-inch (4-cm) cookie cutter in the center of the 2-inch (5-cm) piece of clay. Again, it's worth taking some time to find the correct placement in the center. Press the cookie cutter into the clay and twist a little in both directions. Remove the cutter and circle of clay.

6. Place the outer ring you're left with onto the top of the two piled clay pieces, lining up the inside of the top ring with the inside of the ring below. Gently press it into place with your fingertips. Avoid pressing the edges down to keep them crisp. Blend the join on the inside of the ring with your fingers. Do this gently and carefully so you don't push the circles out of shape.

7. Preheat the oven to 230°F (110°C). Line a foil baking tray with an 8 x 8–inch (20 x 20–cm) piece of parchment paper. Carefully transfer the candleholder to the foil tray. Cover it with a second tray and heat it in the oven for 30 minutes. When the time is up, remove the tray from the oven and leave the clay to cool entirely before lifting it out.

Once the clay has cooled, rub the surface of the clay with wet sandpaper to smooth out any bumps and sharpen the edges. When you're happy with the result, rinse the candleholder in water and dry thoroughly.

Add the tealight inside the metallic wrapper into the hole in the top of the holder.

NATURAL BEADED STRING GARLAND

Garlands are no longer just for hanging. Curl them up and place them directly on a shelf or into a small basket, or carefully lay them across your curated coffee table books. For an effortlessly chic look, always make sure you have a tassel hanging free to get the styling just right.

This piece combines the natural, textured look of air-dry clay with jute twine to create an earthy, organic look. You don't have to be too fussy about shape, size and texture when you're creating the beads—and that gives you more freedom to enjoy the process. This project uses the cooling technique to create holes in each bead. This step isn't essential, but it will help you keep the beads in shape as you push the awl or skewer through them.

materials

30 oz (850 g) white DAS air-dry clay

Baby oil

Parchment paper

10 x 10" (25 x 25–cm) foil baking tray

Awl or skewer

Fine-grain sandpaper

Scissors

Cotton cord

Strong multipurpose glue

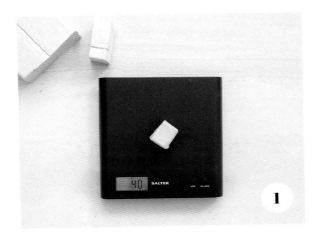

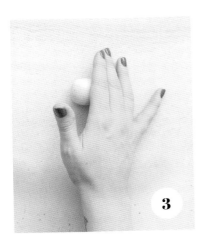

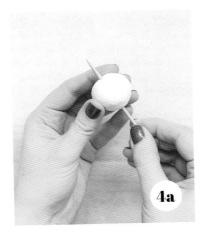

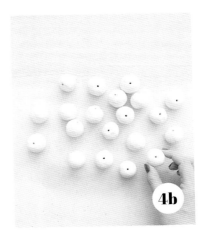

1. Cut twenty 1.5-ounce (42.5-g) pieces of clay, weighing each piece individually to make sure the beads will be roughly the same size.

2. Coat the palms of your hands and fingers in baby oil. Pick up one piece of clay. Roll it between your palms to create a ball.

3. Once you have the rough shape, place the ball on a piece of parchment paper. Place the palm of your hand over the top and roll it gently in circles to get an even sphere. Repeat this process with all of the clay. Place the parchment paper with the clay in a foil baking tray in the freezer for 30 minutes.

4. Gently twist the awl or skewer through the ball of the clay (see image 4a). Take your time to direct the point through the center. When you reach the opposite side, take the skewer out and push it through the hole again from the opposite direction to create a smooth hole through the bead (see image 4b).

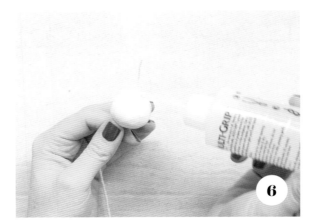

5. Leave the clay in a warm and dry place for 48 hours to dry and set. Lightly sand off any obvious imperfections with the sandpaper. It is difficult and time-consuming to achieve perfect spheres, so don't strive for perfection. You just want to get rid of any obvious flaws that are too distracting.

6. Cut a piece of cord about 40 inches (1 m) long. Tie a large knot at one end of the cord so the first bead cannot pass over it. Add a dab of glue to the knot. When it is dry, cut off the excess cord.

7. Thread all the beads. Tie another knot to hold the beads in place but leave a long tail at the end.

8. Make the tassel by wrapping a piece of cord 120 inches (3 m) long around all the fingers on your hand. Use the end of the cord to wrap them all together about 0.5 inch (1 cm) from one end of the loops. After a couple of loops, tie up the end and push the remaining thread into the middle of the bunch. Now, trim the opposite end from your wrapped cord to create individual threads.

9. Tie the tassel to the extra cord coming from the beads. Make the knot as close to the beads as possible. Trim the excess cord to around 1 inch (2.5 cm) and thread the tail back inside the bead closest to the tassel.

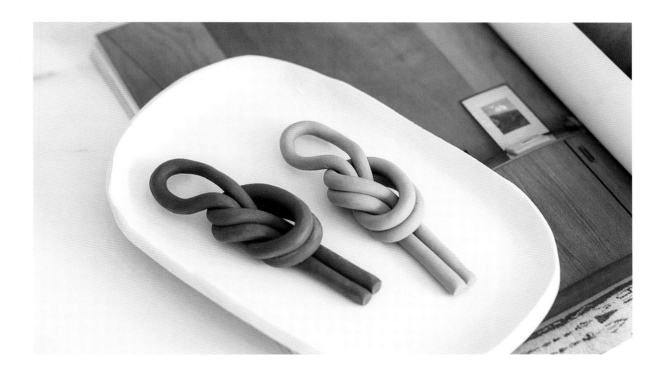

TIE THE KNOT ORNAMENT

Inspiration can come from all around you. This piece is inspired by macramé and knotting, transferring those techniques over to work with the clay. The smooth, flawless knot looks amazing styled on a pile of coffee table books or used as a chic paperweight. We achieve this look by using polymer clay both for its strength and finish—which makes it look anything but handmade. I've used the extruder to create this piece, but it's not essential. Polymer clay rolls easily into tubes, and it's possible to get a smooth, sleek look using just your hands. Take your time rolling with your hands, keeping the pressure even, and always be sure the surface where you roll the clay is clean and dry. If it all goes wrong, just ball up the clay and start again!

materials

1 oz (30 g) taupe or chocolate FIMO polymer clay

Clay extruder

Craft knife

Parchment paper

2 (10 x 10" [25 x 25–cm]) foil baking trays

1. Hold the clay between your palms to warm it. After 30 seconds, begin to work the clay in your hands. Roll it out, twist it together and ball it back up several times until it is soft and pliable. When the clay is warm, start working it together into a ball.

2. Place the clay on a nonstick surface and roll the clay into a tube shape using your hands until the clay is thin enough to fit inside the extruder tube.

3. Twist the lever on the extruder until it has wound the pin out all the way. Squeeze the clay into the extruder, pushing it down until you can't fit any more in. Cut off the excess with a craft knife and cover with the round extruder mold and screw on the cap.

4. Twist the lever on the extruder in the opposite direction. The clay will start to move through the mold and create a long thin tube. Maintain an even speed as you turn the lever and keep the extruder close to the surface, so you don't break the line of clay. You'll need to move the extruder away from the clay slowly as you twist.

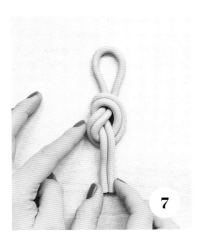

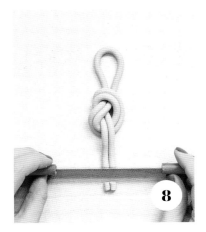

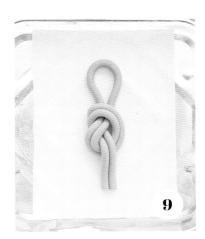

5. Once you have a piece roughly 20 inches (51 cm) long, cut the clay from the extruder and set it to one side. Smooth over the surface of the clay with your fingers to remove any cracks.

6. Gently fold the clay in half with a loop forming at the fold. Don't press this loop together or you will risk bending and breaking the clay.

7. Holding the folded loop in place with one hand, take the two ends and create another loop. Take the two ends under the clay, then back over and through the second loop to make a loose knot.

8. Position the clay tubes neatly so the two strands run side by side throughout the knot and don't cross over. When you're happy with the shape, cut the ends level with a craft knife.

9. Preheat the oven to 230°F (110°C). Line a foil baking tray with an 8 x 8–inch (20 x 20–cm) piece of parchment paper. Transfer the clay to the foil tray and cover it with a second tray. Heat it in the oven for 30 minutes. When the time is up, remove the tray from the oven and leave the clay to cool entirely before lifting it out.

SHIPSHAPE BEADS KEY RING

Sometimes you need a quick craft fix, and this project gives you just that! It's a finished piece you'll love, and you can make it in minutes. These colorful shapes will brighten up your keys and make the daily hunt through your bag much easier! To make the shapes even and symmetrical, you'll need to use cookie cutters for this project. These shape cutters come from a set that I regularly use alongside the full-sized versions. Find them online on Amazon or eBay. As we are not working or conditioning the clay, this project is very quick and easy. It can be harder and more difficult to push the cutter through when you use the clay straight out of the packet. I suggest placing something flat on top of the cutter and applying pressure.

materials

2 oz (57 g) terra-cotta FIMO polymer clay

Small shape cutters: circle, rectangle, triangle

Flat knife

2 (10 x 10" [25 x 25–cm]) foil baking trays

Skewer

2 oz (57 g) champagne FIMO polymer clay

2 oz (57 g) ochre FIMO polymer clay

Parchment paper

Scissors

Thin cotton cord

Key ring

Strong multipurpose glue

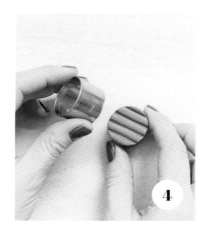

1. Remove the whole terra-cotta clay block from the packet. Make sure there are no cracks in the clay. If you do find any imperfections, smooth over the clay with your finger until it is warm and easily pushed back together.

2. Place the clay, flat side down, on a nonstick surface. Press a small shape cutter into the surface with the palm of your hand. If the clay is too hard to push the cutter through, place a piece of wood over the top of the cutter and apply pressure. Push down until the top of the cutter almost reaches the top of the clay. Break off the pieces outside of the shape cutter away from the surface.

3. Using a flat knife, cut along the bottom of the cutter to remove the extra clay. Place the clay in a baking tray in the freezer for 1 hour.

4. Slowly and gently push the clay back out of the cutter from the top. You don't want to distort the bumpy texture. If this feels soft to the touch, place the cutter and clay into the freezer for 1 hour until it is easier to remove from the cutter without distorting the clay.

5. Smooth over the outside with the knife.

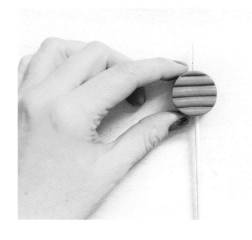

6

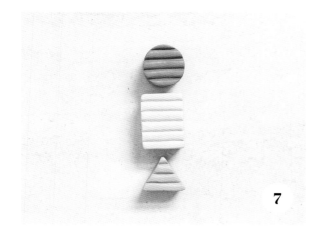

7

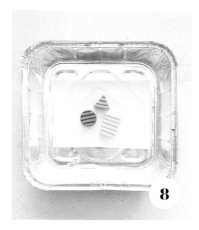

8

9

10

6. Use a skewer to create a hole through the center of the bead. When the skewer reaches the other side of the bead, twist it back out and go back through in the opposite direction. This will ensure the hole is smooth and uniform throughout.

7. Repeat Steps 1 through 6 using the remaining clay colors and cutter shapes.

8. Preheat the oven to 230°F (110°C). Line a foil baking tray with an 8 x 8–inch (20 x 20–cm) piece of parchment paper. Transfer the beads to the foil tray and cover it with a second tray. Heat it in the oven for 30 minutes. When the time is up, remove the tray from the oven and leave the clay to cool entirely before lifting it out.

9. Cut a 40-inch (1-m) length of cord. Thread from the bottom of the last bead up through the other two beads, around the key ring and back down through all the beads.

10. Tie the two ends in a tight knot. Add a dab of glue to the knot and gently pull it inside the bead. Leave this to set in place.

FAUX SPECKLED GLAZE NESTING PLATES

Nesting plates make any surface look more appealing, especially when used on a coffee table to elevate your styling. They are aesthetically pleasing and useful for storing trinkets and jewelry. They are also great for catching crumbs and orange peels—the average day with a toddler.

The speckled glaze is a classic stoneware clay style. But trust me, you won't believe how easy it is to achieve at home with minimal effort. You don't need any special tools or skills and you most likely already have all you need in your kitchen. This magical material is . . . pepper! Yes, cracked pepper. It has an organic tone and texture, and it is completely safe and nontoxic to use. Perfect!

materials

35 oz (1 kg) white DAS air-dry clay

2 (1 x 15 x 0.25" [2.5 x 38 x 0.6–cm]) lengths of wood

Roller

Ruler

Clay carving tool

Craft knife

3 tbsp (20 g) coarsely ground pepper

Parchment paper

Sponge brush or paint brush

Polyurethane water-based varnish

Note: These plates are for decorative purposes only. Do not eat off them or submerge them in water.

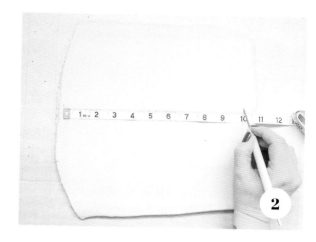

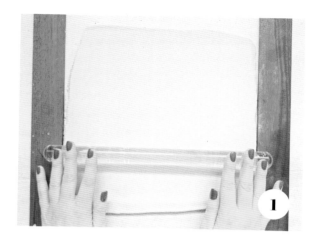

1. Place the clay on a nonstick surface between the two lengths of wood. Roll out the clay until the roller runs smoothly over the clay and it's an even thickness with the wood.

2. Start by making the largest plate in the stack, using the clay carving tool. Measure and place a small mark roughly 10 inches (25 cm) in diameter vertically and horizontally to get the dimensions of the plate.

3. With a craft knife, draw a very rough circle using these points as a guide. The look we're going for is a very imperfect shape; don't worry about making the circle symmetrical. If you are worried about taking the leap with the knife, lightly draw out the circle first, then cut along the line.

4. Remove the clay from outside the circle. Sprinkle the surface of the clay with the ground pepper from a height of about 12 inches (30 cm) to create an irregular pattern.

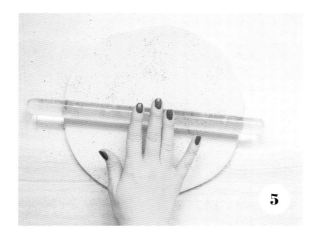

5. Gently roll over the pepper and clay to create a flat surface. Lift the clay at the edge and slide your hand underneath. Transfer the clay to a sheet of parchment paper.

6. Use your fingers and thumbs to lift the edge of the clay around the edge of the circle, creating a lip. Leave the clay to air-dry on a flat surface in a warm room until it sets.

7. Use the sponge brush to apply varnish over the surface. Use two light coats; let the varnish dry completely before starting the second layer. Leave this piece to one side to dry for 24 hours.

8. Make the remaining plates, repeating the steps but measuring the sizes to be 8.5 inches (21.5 cm), 7 inches (18 cm) and 5.5 inches (14 cm). Leave the varnish to dry for 24 hours before stacking.

WALL HANGING POCKET PLANTER

I love the organic look air-dry clay gives a project. It's perfect for these pocket planters, giving them a softer, less polished look that we're seeing in a lot of interior design trends this year.

Using a mixture of varnish and a plastic ziplock bag, you can create a waterproof barrier and protect the clay against the eroding effects of liquids. While your piece will not be completely waterproof, it will take small splashes in stride— making it a great option for succulents and air plants! This project requires some careful joining and blending, so have your tools ready. The trick to a successful join is using an additional piece of clay to make the transition easier.

materials

Letter paper

4.25" (11-cm) circle cookie cutter

Pencil

Scissors

35 oz (1 kg) white DAS air-dry clay

2 (1 x 15 x 0.25" [2.5 x 38 x 0.6–cm]) lengths of wood

Roller

Craft knife

Ruler

Small sponges

Parchment paper

Medium-grain sandpaper

Microfiber cloth

Ziplock bag that fits inside your pot

Strong multi-purpose glue

Dishwasher-safe varnish

Sponge brush or paint brush

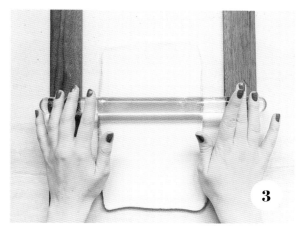

1. Start by making the template for the back of the planter. Fold a piece of paper in half along the width. Place the cookie cutter at one end of the fold so that it is half on the paper and half off over the fold.

Using a pencil, draw around the outside of the cookie cutter onto the paper. Move the cookie cutter to the other end of the paper and repeat. When you have two semicircles along the fold, draw a line between both peaks.

2. Cut along the outer line, ignoring all the marks inside. Unfold the paper and run your finger along the fold to flatten. Now that the template is ready, you can roll out the clay.

3. Place the clay on a nonstick surface between the two lengths of wood. Roll out the clay until the roller runs smoothly over the clay and it's an even thickness with the wood.

4. Place the template over the clay, gently pressing it into position with your fingers. Use the craft knife to cut the clay using the outside of the template as a guide. Be sure you cut away from your other hand to avoid accidents. Remove the clay outside of the template area.

5. Take the template off your clay and fold it in half along the width. Place it back down on the clay, lining up the edge with one half of the oblong.

6. Use the pencil to lightly draw the arch onto the exposed clay. Start by measuring 0.75 inch (2 cm) in from the edge along the folded paper line. Draw a line 3 inches (8 cm) long. Draw an arch connecting the ends of this line. Try to draw the arch so the line stays an equal distance from the edge of the clay.

7. Cut along the lines in the clay with a craft knife and remove the inside piece of clay. Use a wet sponge to smooth over the surface and edges of the clay. Transfer the clay to a piece of parchment paper and place it to one side.

8. Place the remaining clay on a nonstick surface between the two lengths of wood. Roll out the clay until the roller runs smoothly over the clay and it's an even thickness with the wood.

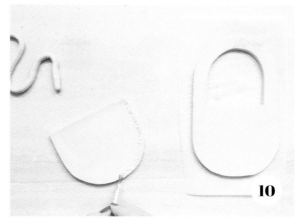

9. Place the folded template over the clay, gently pressing it into position with your fingers. Use the knife to cut the clay using the outside of the template as a guide. Be sure you cut away from your other hand to avoid accidents. Remove the clay outside of the template area and peel off the paper template.

10. Score around the left, right and bottom edge of the clay. Roll up a rough tube shape from the leftover clay and score along one side.

11. Wet both scored areas and press them together, blending the join together with your fingers. Score the top of the tube shape again and the left, right and bottom edge of the first piece of clay.

12. Wet the scored clay and bring the pieces together, placing a sponge in between them for support. Blend the joins and smooth them over using a damp sponge.

13. Leave the clay in a warm, dry place for 24 hours before turning it over and leaving it for another 24 hours until the clay has dried completely and is firm.

14. Use a medium-grain sandpaper to smooth the surface of the clay. Rub the sandpaper over the entire piece, focusing on the joins. Wipe off the clay dust with a damp cloth.

15. Cut the zip section from the top of the ziplock bag. Place the bag in the planter and use a strong glue to secure the top of the bag to the inside of the planter.

16. Cover the rest of the planter with dishwasher-safe varnish. Use the sponge brush to spread three light layers over the surface, leaving each one for 5 hours to fully dry before applying the next.

office

An office doesn't have to feel stuffy and uniform to be a productive space. In fact, I feel more productive in a space that is inspirational and well designed. The key to using clay to organize your space is keeping the overall look minimal while focusing on the function of each piece. In this chapter, we use clay to make your office feel like a professional space with tons of character.

I believe function and decoration should go hand in hand. The She Sells Seashells Magnets (page 60) are this season's must-have design item, bringing your mood board to life or making those important to-do notes look more attractive. The stunning Hourglass Planter (page 82) is deceptively simple to make and gives you the best excuse to go and buy a new plant baby! As well as plants, every office needs artwork. The Terra-Cotta Tile Wall Hanging (page 67) gives you the option to get creative and make a piece of modern art.

But it's not just about decoration. Clay can also be functional in your office, helping you organize your stationery and office supplies and keeping your desk tidy. In this chapter, we will create a range of practical items for the office, from a pencil holder (page 71) that will take you under an hour to make to a modern desk brush (page 91) that will clean your keyboard and look incredibly stylish hanging above your desk.

SHE SELLS SEASHELLS MAGNETS

Mood boards are a fun way to find inspiration and bring together images, quotes, materials, colors and ideas to spark creativity. With this easy magnet project, you can even make your magnets part of your inspiration.

I love shells and terra-cotta, so I've combined the two to create something that adds to the overall theme of my current mood board! I've used air-dry clay for this project, which comes in this fantastic terra-cotta color, so there's no need to paint or dye the clay. Instead, we can focus on creating the shape and definition. You will need to use a mold to create the shell shape. These molds are inexpensive and can be purchased online. Search for "silicone shell mold" and look for a mold that makes a shell shape of around 1 to 1.5 inches (2.5 to 4 cm) high or wide.

materials

10 oz (300 g) terra-cotta DAS air-dry clay

Silicone shell mold

Clay knife

Small circle magnets

Parchment paper

Fine-grain sandpaper

Microfiber cloth

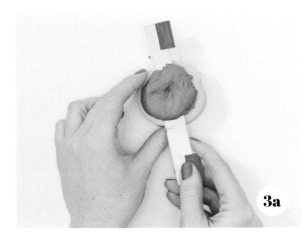

1. Take a piece of clay from the block that looks roughly around the same size as the mold. If you're unsure, take a little more and test it by pushing the clay inside the mold. You should start with more than enough to fill the mold.

Wet your hands with water and roll the clay into a ball using your palms. You want to make sure there are no cracks in the clay both on the inside and outside. Take your time pushing and rolling the clay, using a sprinkle of water when needed to create a smooth surface.

2. Gently push the clay into the mold. Use your thumb to push the clay into all the edges and creases to create the shape. When you can't push the clay down any further, carefully press the outside of the mold back into shape so the shell shape is not stretching and distorting in any direction. This action might cause a bulge of clay to rise out of the mold; that's okay.

3. Use the clay knife to cut off the excess clay from the top of the mold (see image 3a) and smooth the exposed surface of the clay with water (see image 3b).

4

5

6

7

4. Place a magnet on the exposed surface of the clay, positioning it in the center of the shape. Gently push it into clay until both surfaces are aligned.

5. Place the mold in the freezer for 10 minutes to harden the clay, then carefully peel back the mold.

6. Lay the shell, magnet side down, on parchment paper. Leave it in a warm, dry place for 24 hours before turning it over and leaving it for another 24 hours until the clay has dried completely and is firm.

7. Rub the dried clay with sandpaper to refine the shape and smooth the surface. Fold the sandpaper in half and use the fold line to create more definition in the indents of the shell, if needed. Wipe off the dust with a barely wet cloth and leave it to dry again.

FRESH-FACED BOOKEND

This bookend will keep your books neatly collected together, and it also has an added bonus. It's the ideal place to store writing materials, paintbrushes or even your clay tools—whatever makes you happy!

While it might look complicated, don't be fooled by this project! It uses the same technique to build the pot as our planters. We're just changing the shape slightly and adding in this chic, line-drawn detail. The drawing is a simple abstract face, which anyone can re-create; you don't have to be an artist. In fact, the less detail the better, as we need to score and attach the clay along the entire line.

materials

35 oz (1 kg) white DAS air-dry clay

2 (1 x 15 x 0.25" [2.5 x 38 x 0.6–cm]) lengths of wood

Roller

4.25" (11-cm) circle cookie cutter

Craft knife

Parchment paper

Pointed blending tool

Medium-grain sandpaper

Paintbrush or sponge

Beige paint

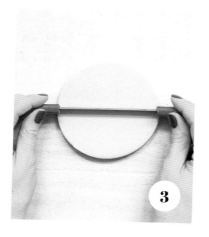
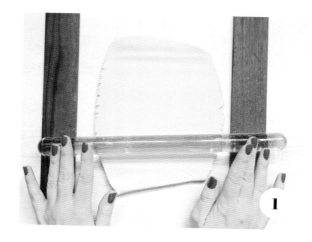
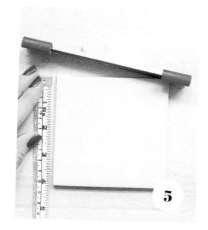

1. Cut off 9 ounces (250 g) of clay. Place the clay on a nonstick surface between the two lengths of wood. Roll out the clay until the roller runs smoothly over the clay and it's an even thickness with the wood.

2. Press the cookie cutter into the surface of the clay, using the flat of your hand to apply even pressure. Twist the cutter slightly in both directions to prevent it from sticking to the clay. Lift the cutter out of the outer piece of clay. Gently press the circle of clay left inside the cutter out to one side on the nonstick surface.

3. Cut the circle in half using a craft knife. Place it to the side on a piece of parchment paper.

4. Take the remaining clay and place it between the two lengths of wood. Cut a rectangle that is 7 x 4.5 inches (18 x 11.5 cm).

5. Wet your hands, ball the remaining clay up and roll it out again. Cut one rectangle that is 4 x 4.5 inches (10 x 11.5 cm).

6. Using a craft knife, gently score along one 4.5-inch (11.5-cm) edge of the smaller rectangle. Score the straight edge of the half circle and press the two scored edges together. Using a blending tool, smooth the join together.

7. Wet your hands and ball up the remaining clay. Roll it into a solid tube shape about 0.13 inch (3 mm) thick and about 16 inches (40 cm) long.

8. Pick up the thin tube of clay and use it to "draw" a face over the 7 x 4.5 inches (18 x 11.5 cm) piece of clay. As you place the clay, gently press down with your fingers. Start with the nose and work up to the eye. Take the clay over the eye like an eyebrow, down the side of the face to the chin and back up to shape the mouth.

9. Once you're happy with the drawing, score the clay underneath the line. Go back over the line and press it more firmly into place, making sure you don't flatten the clay against the pot.

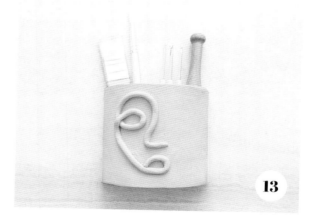

10. Using a craft knife, again gently score along one 7-inch (18-cm) edge and two 4.5-inch (11.5-cm) edges of the larger rectangle. Score the rounded edge of the semicircle. Wet the scored short edge and line it up with the rounded edge of the semicircle, ensuring the sides line up with the outer edges of the pot.

11. Smooth the joins together with your finger or a blending tool, using water to create a seamless join.

12. Leave the pot for 48 hours to set. Once it has dried, sand the piece smooth using a medium-grain sandpaper, then use a small brush to coat the whole piece in two layers of paint. Leave the first coat to dry fully before starting the second coat.

13. Fill the pot with pens, artificial plants, cooking utensils, paintbrushes or anything else you want close at hand.

TERRA-COTTA TILE WALL HANGING

The charm of this project is its rustic look. Clay can look amazing without any surface finishes. While I'm a big advocate for taking the time to polish a completed design, sometimes just leaving the natural finish can be the thing that makes it. The simplicity of this piece makes it a great one to experiment with. Flex those creative muscles and let yourself try something different. If you make a mistake, just ball up the clay, knead it and roll it out again for another try.

materials

14 oz (400 g) terra-cotta DAS air-dry clay

2 (1 x 15 x 0.25" [2.5 x 38 x 0.6–cm]) lengths of wood

Roller

4" (10-cm) circle cookie cutter

Craft knife

Damp sponge

Toothpick or pointed blending tool

Plastic straw

10" (25-cm) piece of cotton cord

Adhesive strip

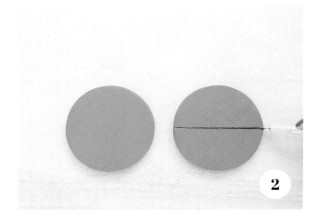

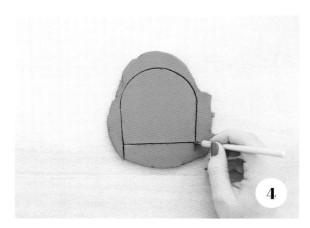

1. Place the clay on a nonstick surface between the two lengths of wood. Roll out the clay until the roller runs smoothly over the clay and it's an even thickness with the wood.

2. Press the cookie cutter into the surface of the clay, using the flat of your hand to apply even pressure. Twist the cutter slightly in both directions to prevent it from sticking to the clay. Lift the cutter out of the outer piece of clay. Gently press the circle of clay left inside the cutter out to one side on the nonstick surface. Cut out two circles from the clay. Cut the second circle in half using a craft knife. Keep one half of the circle; ball up the other half and add it to the rest of the clay.

3. Ball up the remaining clay and place it between the wood. Roll out the clay and gently place the cookie cutter on the surface of the clay. Apply gentle pressure to the clay around the top half of the cookie cutter, then lift it off the clay. You should see a faint line on the clay from the cookie cutter.

4. Use the craft knife to cut a line down from the cut semicircle. Cut a straight line across the bottom of the circle, joining the lines. Remove the excess clay.

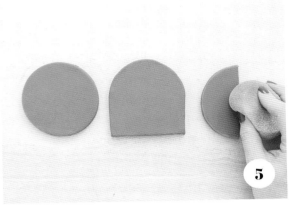

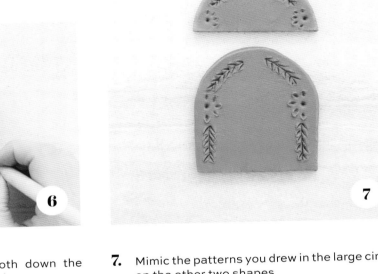

5. Use a damp sponge to smooth down the surface and the sides on each shape.

6. Draw out the design in the clay on the first circle. To help create a symmetrical pattern, start with an element at the north, south, east and west points and work around these. Using a toothpick will give you a sharper, thinner line; the blending tool will create a softer, wider line.

7. Mimic the patterns you drew in the large circle on the other two shapes.

69

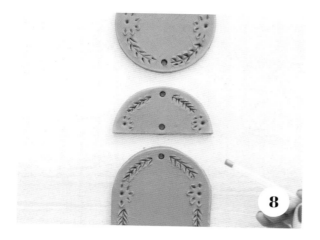

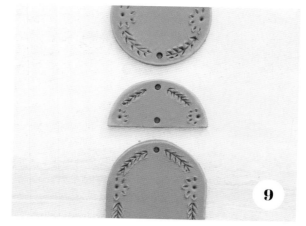

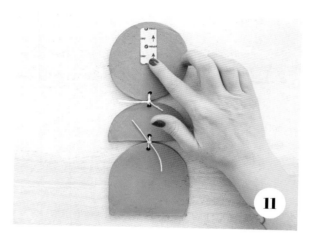

8. Place your pieces of clay in the following order: circle, semicircle, arch. Place the round end of the straw onto the bottom of the first piece of clay, keeping it centered. Push down, twist slightly in both directions and then pull the straw back out. Squeeze the clay from the straw and repeat the process on each piece of clay where the pieces will join. Don't make a hole at the bottom of the last piece of clay.

9. Leave the clay in a warm, dry place to dry for 24 to 48 hours, turning every 12 hours to dry the clay evenly.

10. When the clay is dry, use the cord to tie the pieces of clay together. Make the knots at the back of the piece and cut off the excess cord.

11. Use an adhesive strip to attach the hanging to the wall.

ZIGZAG DESK PENCIL HOLDER

If you're anything like me, the less clutter the better! This pencil holder is a stylish way to keep your work desk organized and minimalist. To create the clean lines needed in this project, the focus is on measuring, cutting and joining. Get these elements right and the rest will fall into place. Pay attention to your joining technique. This is a fantastic opportunity to practice attaching pieces together and blending a seamless join.

materials

35 oz (1 kg) white DAS air-dry clay

2 (1 x 15 x 0.5" [2.5 x 38 x 1.5–cm]) lengths of wood

Roller

Ruler

Craft knife

Parchment paper

10 x 10" (25 x 25–cm) foil baking tray

Blending tool

Medium-grain sandpaper

Fine-grain sandpaper

Microfiber cloth

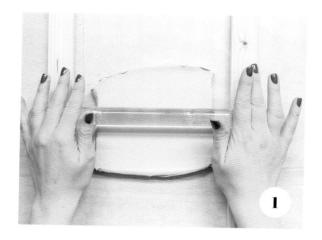

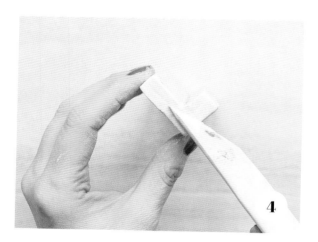

1. Place the clay on a nonstick surface between the two lengths of wood. Roll out the clay until the roller runs smoothly over the clay and it's an even thickness with the wood.

2. Use the ruler and craft knife to measure and cut seven pieces of clay, each 1 x 6 inches (2.5 x 15.25 cm). If you run out of clay, wet your hands, ball up the clay and start again. Place the pieces on a piece of parchment paper in a foil baking tray. Place them in the freezer for 1 hour.

3. Remove the clay from the freezer. Take one piece in your left hand and score along one of the long sides, adding a little water. Line up this scored side with the top of another piece along the left edge. This should create a V shape at a right angle.

4. Stand the clay on the shorter edges and blend the join with a blending tool or your fingers on the three visible sides. Use a little water to help smooth over the line where the two pieces join together and create a seamless shape.

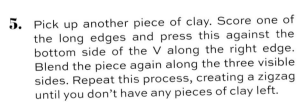

5. Pick up another piece of clay. Score one of the long edges and press this against the bottom side of the V along the right edge. Blend the piece again along the three visible sides. Repeat this process, creating a zigzag until you don't have any pieces of clay left.

6. Leave the clay to dry for 4 to 6 hours, then carefully turn the clay over 180 degrees. Blend the joins along the top edge, adding water to help create a smooth surface.

7. Leave the clay to dry for 48 hours. Sand over the surface with a medium-grain sandpaper, focusing on creating a crisp edge. When the clay is smooth, sand it again with a fine-grain sandpaper. Use a damp cloth to wipe the surface of the clay and remove the powdered clay.

SNAIL MAIL LETTER HOLDER

I'm always looking for cute solutions to everyday problems. If you have stacks of paperwork waiting on your desk, make this letter holder and say good-bye to the clutter. Organize your letters, receipts and documents into handy sections, easy to access at a moment's notice.

This project explores structure and stability, taking you through a technique that helps strengthen joins and holds the clay in place while it sets. It also helps to stop breakages and cracking when we're using the clay on a regular basis.

materials

3.5 oz (100 g) terra-cotta DAS air-dry clay

35 oz (1 kg) white DAS air-dry clay

Roller

2 (1 x 15 x 0.5" [2.5 x 38 x 1.5–cm]) lengths of wood

Ruler

Clay slicer tool

Parchment paper

Damp sponge

2 (1 x 15 x 0.25" [2.5 x 38 x 0.6–cm]) lengths of wood

4.25" (11-cm) circle cookie cutter

Craft knife

3.75" (9.5-cm) circle cookie cutter

3.25" (8-cm) circle cookie cutter

2.5" (6-cm) circle cookie cutter

2" (5-cm) circle cookie cutter

Toothpicks

Scissors

Blending tool

Fine-grain sandpaper

1. Start by mixing the clay together. Roll the terra-cotta clay into a rough tube shape and lay it on top of the white clay. With a roller, start working the clay together by rolling back and forth over the clay. Once the clay is around half its original depth, start to use your hands to mix the clay. Use your hands to roll it into a tube shape, twist, pull and ball up the clay. Keep repeating this method until the clay is a solid and consistent color.

2. Place the clay on a nonstick surface between the 0.5-inch (1.5-cm)-thick lengths of wood. Roll out the clay until the roller runs smoothly over the clay and it's an even thickness with the wood.

3. Measure and mark a square piece of clay 4 x 6 inches (10 x 15 cm) in size. Using a clay slicer tool, cut along the lines you just made. It helps to hold a ruler or straight piece of wood along the clay to guide you as you cut.

4. Remove the clay from outside the square, roll it into a ball and put it to one side. Carefully lift the edges of the square and slide your hand underneath. Transfer the square of clay to a piece of parchment paper. Use a damp sponge to smooth over the surface of the clay.

5. Take the ball of clay and place it between two pieces of 0.25-inch (0.6-cm)-thick wood. Roll out the clay until the roller runs smoothly over the clay and it's an even thickness with the wood. Take the largest cookie cutter and press it into the surface of the clay, using the flat of your hand to apply even pressure. Twist the cutter slightly in both directions to prevent it from sticking to the clay. Lift the cutter out of the outer piece of clay. Gently press the circle of clay left inside the cutter out to one side on the nonstick surface. Cut the clay circle in half with a craft knife and bring one side of the circle back to your pile of working clay.

6. Repeat this process to create the five semicircles, one in each size from large to small. Ball and reroll the clay as needed. Use a damp sponge to smooth the surface of the semicircles, ensuring the edges and both sides are smooth and free from cracks and imperfections.

7. We're going to use toothpicks to stabilize the semicircles on the square surface of clay. Start with the smallest semicircle. Gently push one toothpick into the middle of the straight edge, pushing up to the peak of the rounded edge. Cut the toothpick with scissors to leave just under 0.5 inch (1.5 cm) of the toothpick protruding from the semicircle.

8. Place one toothpick into the second smallest semicircle. For the other three semicircles, use three toothpicks, pushing one into the center of the straight edge and the other two into either side of the center.

9. Measure 3 inches (7.5 cm) from one edge of the square piece of clay. Take the smallest semicircle and line up the toothpick with this line at the very front of the square. When you push the toothpick into the clay, you want the semicircle to sit in line with the edge of the square piece of clay. Push the toothpick into the square piece of clay. Using your finger or a blending tool, smooth over the join to create a seamless surface.

10. Measure 0.75 inch (2 cm) along the square from this first semicircle. Make a small mark around the center to help guide you. Now measure 3 inches (7.5 cm) from the side of the square. Where the two marks meet is where you need to line up the center toothpick. Push this into the clay again and blend the joins. It's helpful here to have a blending tool for difficult-to-reach parts of the clay.

11. Repeat Step 10 with the other three semicircles. Your final semicircle should line up with the back edge of the square. You can adjust the distance between the semicircles slightly to allow for any discrepancies in previous measurements.

12. Leave the clay to dry for 48 hours. Use a fine-grain sandpaper to even out the surface of the clay and define the edges. Rub the sandpaper back and forth over the thin edges of each semicircle to create a smooth and crisp edge.

ON A ROLL CLAY PLANTER

Bored of your old planters? Give them a fun and eye-catching makeover with air-dry clay. This project is much easier than it looks. Layering up the clay rolls creates a playful shape that's huge in interior design and pottery trends right now. Get ready to roll, because this project is all about creating even tubes of clay to stack. Once you've nailed the technique, you'll have this pot made in minutes! You can use any size round planter, but smaller pots are best to start with. Just ensure you have enough clay to create pieces long enough to wrap around the planter. Measure the circumference and add an extra inch (2.5 cm).

materials

70 oz (2 kg) white DAS air-dry clay	Medium-grain sandpaper
Baby oil	Fine-grain sandpaper
Ruler	
Clay slicer tool	Microfiber cloth
Round plant pot (12.5" [32-cm] circumference)	Paintbrush
	Latex paint
Parchment paper	Dishwasher-safe varnish
Pointed clay tool	
Makeup sponge	Sponge brush or paint brush
Strong multi-purpose glue	

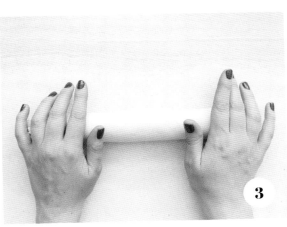

1. Weigh out 17.5 ounces (500 g) of clay. Coat your hands in baby oil and squeeze the clay into a slightly rounded shape to make it easier to roll.

2. Place the clay on a large nonstick surface so you are looking at it horizontally. Roll out the clay into a solid tube shape. Start by placing your fingertips on the clay. Push your hands forward, rolling the clay underneath them on the surface until you reach the bottom of your palms. Then bring your hands back toward you, never losing contact with the clay.

3. Continue this action, moving your hands along the entire length of the tube to create an even pressure as you roll. This should help you create an even shape. This might take some practice to get perfect; remember you can easily ball up the clay and start again. Just be sure the clay does not dry out by adding small amounts of water as you're working with it.

4. As you roll the clay, keep measuring the length until you reach 14 inches (35 cm). You need to roll an additional 0.5 inch (1.5 cm) at both ends of the tube so that you can cut the excess off with a clay slicer tool and create a straight, flat edge that's an even thickness with the rest of the shape.

5. Place the planter on a sheet of parchment paper. Gently lift the clay tube and wrap it around the bottom of the planter so it is touching all the way around. You should have some excess clay. Place one end of the clay on top of the other and cut through both at the same point. Score both of the flat ends with a pointed clay tool and dab a little water on with your finger.

6. Using your finger and a little water, blend the join together to create a seamless join.

7. Repeat Steps 1 through 6: Roll out another three pieces of clay and add them to the planter, placing each one on top of the last. Blend the joins together and, when all the clay is in place, use a damp makeup sponge to smooth the surface of the clay.

8. Leave the clay to harden in a warm, dry place for 48 to 72 hours. When it is dry, very gently remove the planter from the inside of the clay rolls. Add glue to the surface of the planter. You don't need too much, but be sure you have a little glue around the entire circumference of the pot.

9. Place the planter back inside the rolls of clay and leave it to dry for 12 hours.

10. Sand the surface of the clay: Start with the medium-grain sandpaper, gently rubbing the flat surface over the curves of clay. Fold the sandpaper in half and run this along the space where the two rolls of clay meet. Repeat this process with the fine-grain sandpaper. Use a damp cloth to remove the powdered clay left from sanding and leave it to dry.

11. Use the paintbrush to paint the clay, pushing the paint into the crease between rolls. Keep the layers light, building them up to create a solid color. Wait for each layer to dry before starting the next.

12. When the paint is dry, cover the clay in dishwasher-safe varnish using the sponge brush. This will protect the surface from any splashes of water. Use two light coats; let the varnish dry completely before starting the second layer. Leave the varnish to dry overnight.

HOURGLASS PLANTER

I have such an obsession with hourglass planters. They are usually much larger than this one, but I decided to try out a miniature version, and it is beyond cute! The hourglass shape is a modern twist on the traditional planter, which you'll create from two separately molded pieces.

This planter looks great with striking succulents, such as a Zebra Plant (*Haworthia attenuata*), or with small trailing plants, such as a String of Pearls or Burrow's Tail. For a pop of color and fresh green vibes while I'm working, it will take a place of pride on my desk next to my computer. But the planter is versatile enough to work anywhere in your home. It could be a great bathroom piece or a fun accent on a shelving unit.

materials

70 oz (2 kg) terra-cotta DAS air-dry clay

Large breakfast bowl (5.5" [13-cm] diameter)

Baby oil

Wire-cutting tool (optional)

Craft knife

Parchment paper

Damp sponge

Wire clay carving tool

Toothpick

Ruler

Medium-grain sandpaper

Fine-grain sandpaper

Microfiber cloth

Dishwasher-safe varnish

Sponge brush or paint brush

Strong multi-purpose glue

Ziplock bag that fits inside your pot

Soil, plant and perlite to fill the pot

1. Weigh out 44 ounces (1.25 kg) of terra-cotta air-dry clay. Roll it up into a rough ball shape. Using wet hands, smooth over the surface of the clay.

2. Coat the inside of the bowl with a layer of baby oil. Place the clay ball in the bowl and, using your fingers, push down so the clay fills the bowl and the top is flat. Depending on the size of your bowl, you might need to add clay to fill it or cut off the extra clay with a wire-cutting tool.

3. Use water to smooth over the flat exposed surface of the clay. Run your nail around the edge of the bowl to stop the clay from running over the lip and place the bowl in a warm, dry place. Leave the clay to set for 12 hours.

4. After 12 hours, turn the bowl upside down onto a wood surface, lift it slightly off the surface and shake. Air-dry clay shrinks as it dries, so your clay should be easy to remove from the bowl. The clay should come loose as you shake it. If it does not, run a craft knife around the top of the bowl between the clay and the bowl.

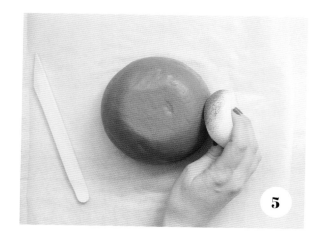

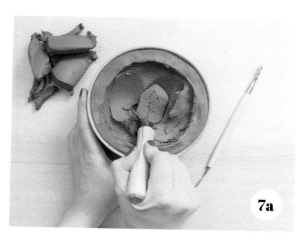

5. Place the clay on a piece of parchment paper and smooth over the surface of the clay with a damp sponge. Leave this to dry for 48 to 72 hours.

6. Repeat Steps 1 and 2 with the remaining clay. Draw a circle in the clay 0.5 inch (1.5 cm) from the edge using the bowl as a guide.

7. Using the wire clay carving tool, start to carve out the clay inside this circle (see image 7a). The aim is to leave an inch (2.5 cm) around the edge of the clay, so as you get deeper into the bowl carve at the same angle as the sides. If you notice you have carved away too much clay, it's easy to add in more (see image 7b). Leave about 1 inch (2.5 cm) at the bottom of the bowl. Check this measurement by pushing a toothpick into the clay until it reaches the hard surface of the bowl. Hold the toothpick between your fingers at the clay line and pull it out. Measure the distance between your fingers and the end of the toothpick to find out how thick the clay is. Remember you can always add more clay if it's too thin.

Leaving the clay inside the bowl, smooth over the exposed surface with a damp sponge. Be sure the top edge is smooth and free from imperfections. Leave the clay to set for 12 hours.

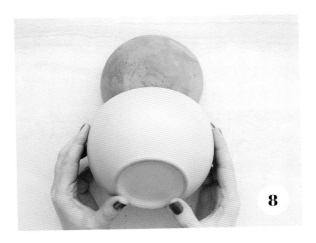

8. Turn the bowl upside down onto a wood surface, lift it slightly off the surface and shake. The clay should come loose as you shake it. If it does not, run a craft knife around the top of the bowl between the clay and the bowl.

9. Place the clay onto a piece of parchment paper and smooth over the surface of the clay with a damp sponge. Leave this to dry for 48 to 72 hours.

10. Sand the entire surface of both pieces of clay: Start with the medium-grain sandpaper, gently rubbing it over the surface in small circles. Brush away the powdered clay that remains. Sand again with a fine-grain sandpaper to create a smooth surface texture.

11. Depending on the shape of your bowl, you might need to sand the top of the dome flat. You'll need a flat edge of around 2 inches (5 cm) on both pieces of clay. This is easy to do with the medium-grain sandpaper.

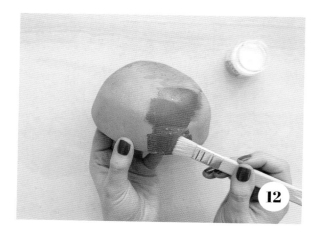

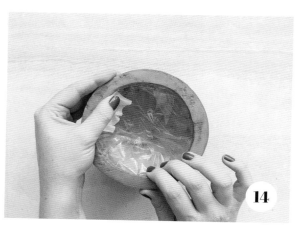

12. Wipe away the powdered clay with a damp cloth and leave the clay to dry for 10 to 15 minutes. When the surface is dry, coat it with three thin layers of dishwasher-safe varnish using a sponge brush. Wait for each layer to dry before starting the next. This should take about 1 hour, but it might be longer depending on the conditions where you are.

13. Once the varnish is dry, turn the solid half sphere so it's sitting on the flat side. Add a generous amount of glue to the flat top of the dome and place the flat top of the second piece of clay on top. Push it down and wipe away any excess glue before it dries.

14. Leave the glue to dry for around 6 hours. Place the ziplock in the hole at the top of the planter. Cut the bag along the line of the top of the planter. Take the bag back out and run a bead of glue along the inside of the planter about 0.5 inch (1.5 cm) away from the top. Replace the bag and press the edge against the glue. You don't want the bag to be visible over the top of the clay. If there's any excess plastic, fold it and use the glue to secure it to the rest of the bag.

15. When the glue is dry, fill the planter with soil and your plant. Cover the surface of the soil with perlite to help hide the bag.

HANDS-ON LETTER OPENER

We all need a helping hand every now and then. This letter opener makes paying the bills a little bit easier and gives us a design statement we can all get behind! While making this piece, you'll explore carving and shaping on a smaller scale to create something more intricate. This simple hand shape is easy to replicate and cut with a craft knife before using your hands and tools to smooth and refine the shape.

materials

3 oz (85 g) dolphin grey FIMO polymer clay

2 (1 x 15 x 0.25" [2.5 x 38 x 0.6–cm]) lengths of wood

Roller

Toothpick or pointed clay tool

Ruler

Craft knife

Clay slicer tool

Parchment paper

Blending tool

2 (10 x 10" [25 x 25–cm]) foil baking trays

Medium-grain wet-or-dry sandpaper

Fine-grain wet-or-dry sandpaper

Microfiber cloth

Polyurethane water-based varnish

Sponge brush or paint brush

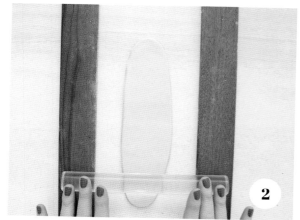

1. Hold the clay between your palms to warm it. After 30 seconds, begin to work the clay in your hands. Roll it out, twist it together and ball it back up several times until it is soft and pliable.

2. Place the clay on a nonstick surface between the lengths of wood. Roll out the clay in one direction into a long rectangle until the roller runs smoothly over the clay and it's an even thickness with the wood.

3. Using a toothpick, draw a very simple hand at the top of the clay. Make the hand roughly 2 inches (5 cm) long with a gap of about 0.5 inch (1.5 cm) where the wrist should be. Don't worry if you make a mistake; you can always start again. You can also practice drawing your hand on paper for some extra confidence. Remember, it doesn't have to be perfect.

4. Measure a distance of 6 inches (15 cm) away from the bottom of the hand and make a small mark. Using the straight edge of a ruler as a guide, draw two lines coming from the wrist of the hand down to the mark you just made.

5. Remove the ruler and taper one of the lines until it meets the other, starting about an inch (2.5 cm) from your mark.

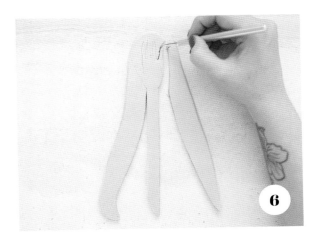

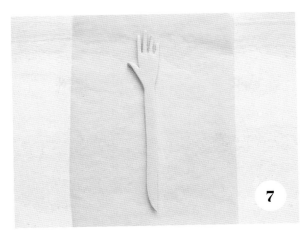

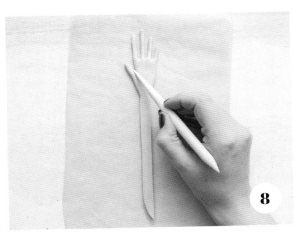

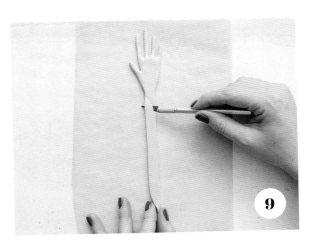

6. Use a craft knife to slowly and carefully cut the line in the clay. Make sure the blade in the knife is sharp to ensure the details are clean and crisp. Work around the curves of the hand. I find it helps to cut away excess clay and then go back in to define the curves. Don't worry if the rounder shapes aren't perfect at this point; we'll address that in a later step.

7. Once the additional clay has been removed, carefully slide the clay slicer tool underneath the long piece of clay and gently lift it from the surface. Place it down on a piece of parchment paper.

8. Use a small blending tool to smooth the clay around the hand shape, focusing on the tips of the fingers, in between the fingers and the outer edge of the palm. Gently stroke the surface of the clay with the tool to smooth the clay. If the clay is cold and hard to blend, hold your hand on the area for 1 minute to warm it and try again.

9. To create a sharper edge on the knife, run the craft knife along the edge of the curved side at a 45-degree angle. Start from the tip and stop around 1 inch (2.5 cm) away from the hand. Use the blending tool to create a softer transition into the pointed edge along the length of the clay.

10. Preheat the oven to 230°F (110°C). Transfer the parchment paper to a foil baking tray and cover it with a second tray. Heat it in the oven for 30 minutes. When the time is up, remove the tray from the oven and leave the clay to cool entirely before lifting it out.

11. When the clay is cool, cut off and wet a small strip of the medium-grain sandpaper with some water. Firmly rub the edges around the piece until they feel smooth. Fold the sandpaper over the tapered edge and press your fingers and thumb over it firmly. Run the sandpaper up and down the length until the edge comes to a defined point.

12. Take a piece of the fine-grain sandpaper and wet it with some water. Hold this down on a flat surface with your fingers and thumb at opposite ends of the strip. With your other hand, rub the clay over the surface of the sandpaper. Sand evenly over the entire surface of the clay.

13. Rinse the clay with water and dry it with a cloth. Coat the clay in two thin layers of varnish using a sponge brush, allowing the first coat to fully dry before applying the second. When the first side is dry, turn the piece over and varnish the other side.

MINI DESK BRUSH

Is it just me or is cleaning easier when you have beautifully designed tools to do it with? This little brush is so aesthetically pleasing, you'll never have to hide it with the rest of the cleaning products. While I love anything that looks good on a shelf, the real bonus is having a brush so close to hand for dust, crumbs and those creative messes you're making with your clay!

The bristles in this brush are, would you believe, made from an inexpensive paintbrush. They are perfect because they hold up against use and are strong enough to flick dirt and debris. Cut long bristles from a paintbrush and keep them wrapped with an elastic band until you need them.

materials

1 lb (450 g) white DAS air-dry clay

2 (1 x 15 x 1" [2.5 x 38 x 2.5–cm]) lengths of wood

Roller

Clay slicer tool

3.5" (9-cm) circle cookie cutter

Parchment paper

Damp sponge

Awl

Masking tape

Fine-grain sandpaper

Paintbrush bristles (removed from a paintbrush)

Small elastic bands

Strong multipurpose glue

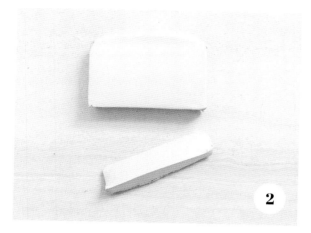

1. Place the clay on a nonstick surface between the two lengths of wood. Roll this out until the roller runs smoothly over the clay and it's an even thickness with the wood.

2. Use a clay slicer tool to cut one end of the clay straight.

3. Place the cookie cutter on the surface of the clay and position it so it's half off and half on. Apply even pressure. Once the cutter has gone through the clay, twist it in both directions two to three times and lift out. Remove the excess clay and, if necessary, gently push the clay circle out of the cutter.

4. Place the circle on a piece of parchment paper and smooth every surface with a damp sponge. Carefully lift the clay to turn and access each side as you do this.

5. Place the clay back down on one semicircle side. Make twelve marks with the awl along the straight flat side of the clay in two evenly spaced rows of six.

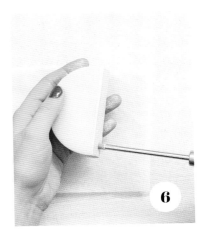

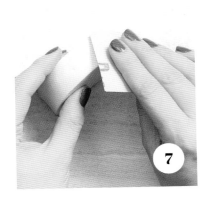

6. Wrap a piece of masking tape around the awl 0.75 inch (2 cm) from the tip and use this as a guide. Push the awl around 0.75 inch (2 cm) into the clay at each of the twelve markings, ensuring each hole is the same size. After all the holes are made, smooth again with the sponge.

7. Leave the clay to dry in a warm place for 48 hours. Once it's dry, sand the entire surface with sandpaper, rubbing the surface in small circles until it is smooth and free from bumps or rough areas.

8. Separate the bristles into twelve even piles. The piles should be about the same size as the holes made in the clay with the awl. Tap the end of the bristles on a flat surface to create an even line and wrap with a small elastic band.

9. Squeeze a generous amount of glue into one of the holes (see image 9a) and place the end of one group of bristles into the hole (see image 9b). Make sure you can easily remove the elastic band later.

10. Repeat the last step until all the holes are filled with bristles. Leave the brush for 24 hours to ensure the glue has set. Remove the elastic bands carefully.

ABSTRACT PLANTER

Whether you're a color addict or like to keep calm with neutrals, abstract patterns will work with your decor choices. See this project as an opportunity to experiment and have fun. With these techniques, you'll never create the exact same piece twice, so embrace the unpredictable nature of the clay and enjoy the process. You can carefully curate your color combinations or use up leftover pieces of clay for something more surprising. I never throw my offcuts away; I store them in ziplock bags until I have enough for a project like this one. I pick out the colors that I feel go well together and give myself some creative freedom to experiment.

The trick to a smooth, consistent surface is rolling until you cannot see the join between the clay colors. Don't blend, as we want a crisp, sharp line. Play with layering, size, shape and color to create miniature pieces of art for your lucky plants!

materials

1 lb (450 g) leaf green FIMO polymer clay

1.75 oz (50 g) black FIMO polymer clay

Roller

2 (1 x 15 x 0.25" [2.5 x 38 x 0.6–cm]) lengths of wood

3.5" (9-cm) circle cookie cutter

2 (1 x 15 x 0.13" [2.5 x 38 x 0.3–cm]) lengths of wood

1.75 oz (50 g) windsor blue FIMO polymer clay

1.75 oz (50 g) peach FIMO polymer clay

1.75 oz (50 g) antique rose FIMO polymer clay

Ruler

Craft knife

Flat blending tool

2 (10 x 10" [25 x 25–cm]) foil baking trays

Parchment paper

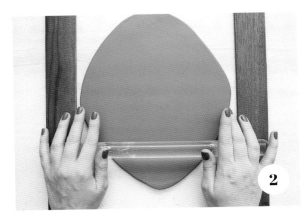

1. Mix the leaf green clay with the black. Break the large green piece into four pieces and warm each one in the palms of your hands. Use the roller to roll it out as thin as you can. This might be difficult as you have not worked the clay soft yet; don't worry if you can't roll it out too thinly. Break the black clay into four roughly even pieces. Add one of each to your four green blocks. Warm each block between your palms once again. Start rolling it into a tube, then back into a ball several times until the clay feels soft and malleable and the colors are mixed together. When it is ready, add the next piece of clay and repeat the process until all the clay is in one ball and shows a solid color.

2. Place the clay on a nonstick surface between two lengths of 0.25-inch (0.6-cm)-thick wood. Roll it out until the roller runs smoothly over the clay and it's an even thickness with the wood.

3. Press the cookie cutter into the surface of the clay, using the flat of your hand to apply even pressure. Twist the cutter slightly in both directions to prevent it from sticking to the clay. Lift the cutter out of the outer piece of clay. Gently press the circle of clay left inside the cutter out to one side on the nonstick surface.

4. Roll the leftover piece back into a ball and place it between the two 0.13-inch (0.3-cm)-thick lengths of wood. Roll out the clay until the roller runs smoothly over both the clay and the wood, creating an even thickness throughout the clay.

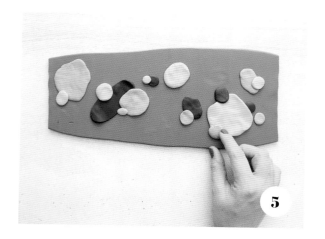

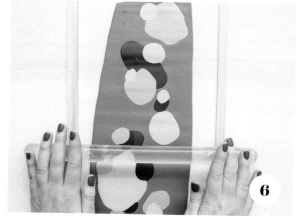

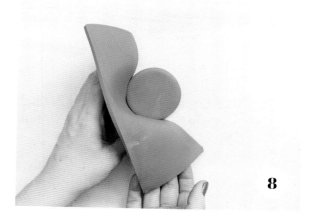

5. Break different-sized pieces off the blue, peach and antique rose clay. Warm these between your palms and roll them until soft and smooth. Squeeze the pieces between your fingers and place them at random on the rolled-out green clay. You can overlap, place next to or separate the pieces to create interesting visual effects.

6. Once the clay is all in place, roll back over the clay using the 0.13-inch (0.3-cm)-thick lengths of wood as a guide.

7. Measure and cut a rectangular piece of clay that is 11.5 x 3.5 inches (29.25 x 9 cm).

8. Wrap the longer edge around the circle piece of clay. Carefully line up the long edge with the bottom of the clay circle.

9. Bring the two shorter edges of the rectangle together so they meet along the 0.13-inch (0.3-cm) side. Push them together gently.

10. Warm the clay on both sides of the join with your fingers, then use a flat blending tool to blend the clay along the join on both the outside and inside.

11. Preheat the oven to 230°F (110°C). Line a foil baking tray with an 8 x 8–inch (20 x 20–cm) piece of parchment paper. Carefully transfer the pot to the foil tray and cover it with a second tray. Heat it in the oven for 30 minutes. When the time is up, remove the tray from the oven and leave the clay to cool entirely before lifting it out.

bedroom

The bedroom is a place of calm and rest, but it's also a place where we need storage and function to go about our everyday lives. In fact, the bedroom is an incredibly hardworking space and has a huge effect on our well-being. If we start the day with small elements around us that are pleasing, it can create a more positive influence on our mood. This is why I put more time and energy into my bedroom decor than any other space in my home. I love using clay to create accents that bring me joy and, at the same time, have a purpose to make the most of the space.

In this chapter, I share great ways to create beautiful accessories that will slot into your regular routines and elevate the mood around you. The Cream Cone Reed Diffuser (page 104) is a simple thing of beauty. It's an easy project that shows you how to use templates to create more interesting shapes. We also use a template to create the Catchall Tray (page 114), which is a great example of how to sculpt a rounded shape without using a mold.

We also play with color in this chapter—from applying color and pattern as a finish to bringing colors together in an abstract way to create recognizable finishes.

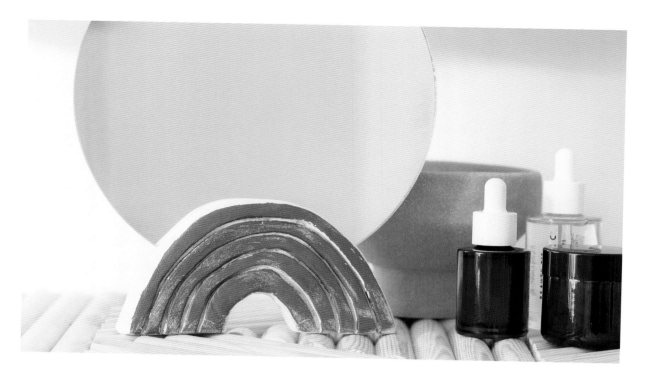

RAINBOW VANITY MIRROR BASE

This vanity mirror stand gives a nod to the popular rainbow trend. The earthy colors and imperfect lines create more subtle tones, resulting in a more grown-up piece that injects a boho vibe in your vanity. You'll love looking at this mirror morning, noon and night!

This rustic look is simple to re-create. It's much easier to work in this style when working without molds or templates. Rather than trying to create perfect symmetry or a flawless texture, embrace the uneven nature of the clay for this project. You'll love the results!

materials

35 oz (1 kg) white DAS air-dry clay

Baby oil

Sponge

Parchment paper

Roller

Clay slicer tool

Pointed clay tool

Circle mirror

Medium-grain sandpaper

Fine-grain sandpaper

Microfiber cloth

Paintbrush

Latex paint

Toothpick (optional)

Strong multipurpose glue

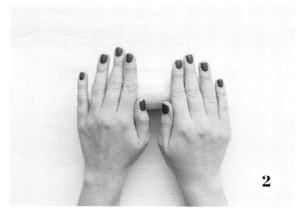

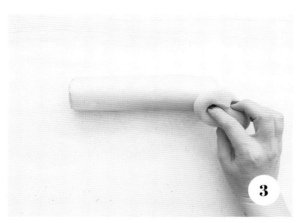

1. Weigh out 17.5 ounces (500 g) of clay. Coat your hands in baby oil and squeeze the clay into a slightly rounded shape to make it easier to roll.

2. Place the clay on a large nonstick surface so you are looking at it horizontally. Roll out the clay into a solid tube shape. Start by placing your fingertips on the clay. Push your hands forward, rolling the clay underneath them on the surface until you reach the bottom of your palms. Then bring your hands back toward you, never losing contact with the clay.

3. Continue this action, moving your hands along the entire length of the tube to create an even pressure as you roll. This should help you create an even shape. Roll the clay until you have a piece 8 inches (20 cm) long. This might take some practice to get perfect; remember, you can easily ball up the clay and start again. Just be sure the clay does not dry out by adding small amounts of water and smoothing it with a sponge as you're working with it.

4. Cut two pieces of parchment paper larger than the shape you have made. Place one down on your nonstick surface and lift the clay on the paper. Hold either side of the clay tube and bend them both toward you to create an arch.

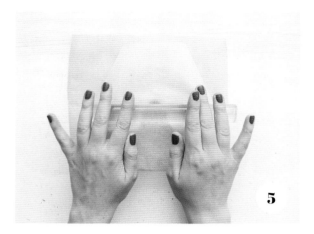

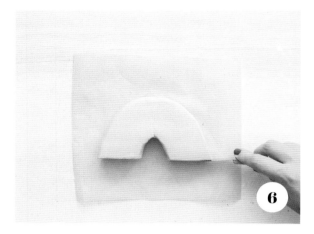

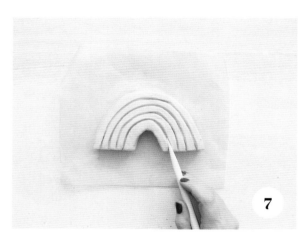

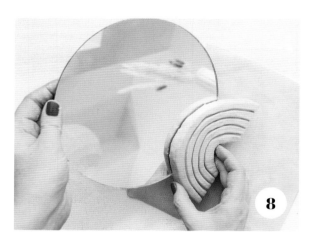

5. Lay the other piece of paper over the top of the clay and gently roll with the roller. Take care to keep the clay a roughly even thickness. Roll it out until you have a piece 2 inches (5 cm) thick.

6. Peel off the top piece of parchment paper. Use the clay slicer tool to cut through both ends of the arch to create a flat edge the piece will eventually sit on.

7. Use the pointed clay tool to draw the lines of the arch on the front of the clay. Follow the lines of the outer edge, staying roughly the same distance from the edge along the line. Make the marks around 0.25 inch (6 mm) deep.

8. Lift up the back of the piece and place it down on the legs/bottom of the arches so it stands as an arch. Press the mirror into the top of the arch to create the right-sized slot for the mirror to sit in. Press it down into the clay until you can let go and it will stay in place. Remove the mirror and place to one side.

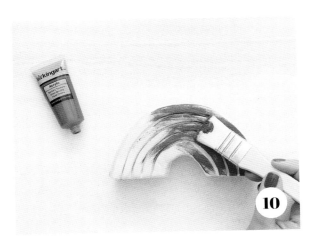

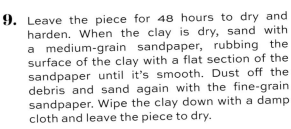

9. Leave the piece for 48 hours to dry and harden. When the clay is dry, sand with a medium-grain sandpaper, rubbing the surface of the clay with a flat section of the sandpaper until it's smooth. Dust off the debris and sand again with the fine-grain sandpaper. Wipe the clay down with a damp cloth and leave the piece to dry.

10. Using a dry brush, paint over the front of the piece. Use a small amount of paint on the brush as you paint over the indented lines to stop the paint from seeping inside. If any paint does find its way into the indents, you can scratch it out with a toothpick. Paint the rest of the piece and leave it to dry for 6 hours.

11. Add a little glue to the bottom of the mirror and press it back into the hole in the top of the clay stand. Leave this to dry so the mirror is secured in the stand.

CREAM CONE REED DIFFUSER

This is such a fun play on shape, and it shows how versatile clay can be. The key to creating the perfect cone is cutting the clay to the right size. Your template is an important tool. You'll need to use it to cut the clay and to create a sturdy surface to blend the joins of the cone.

I use an online cone template maker whenever I need to make a cone shape. Just input the details from the materials list and create the cone. Print it out and cut around the template. This is an easy way to get the perfect cone every time.

materials

5 oz (150 g) champagne FIMO polymer clay

2 (1 x 15 x 0.25" [2.5 x 38 x 0.6–cm]) lengths of wood

Roller

2.75" (7-cm) circle cookie cutter

Cone template:

- Top diameter: 0.75" (2 cm)
- Bottom diameter: 3.25" (8 cm)
- Height: 3.25" (8 cm)

Craft knife

Parchment paper

2 (10 x 10" [25 x 25–cm]) foil baking trays

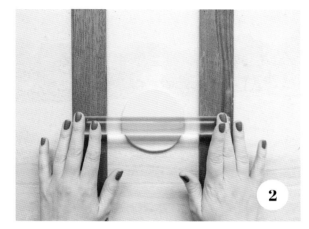

1. Weigh out 1.5 ounces (50 g) of clay. Hold the clay between your palms to warm the clay. After 30 seconds, begin to work the clay in your hands. Roll it out, twist it together and ball it back up several times until it is soft and pliable.

2. Place the clay on a nonstick surface between the lengths of wood. Roll out the clay until the roller runs smoothly over the clay and it's an even thickness with the wood.

3. Press the cookie cutter into the surface of the clay, using the flat of your hand to apply even pressure. Twist the cutter slightly in both directions to prevent it from sticking to the clay. Lift the cutter out of the outer piece of clay. Gently press the circle of clay left inside the cutter out to one side on the nonstick surface.

4. Add the excess clay to the remaining 3.5 ounces (100 g) of clay. Warm and work this in your hands until it is soft. Place the clay between the lengths of wood. Roll out the clay until the roller runs smoothly over the clay and it's an even thickness with the wood.

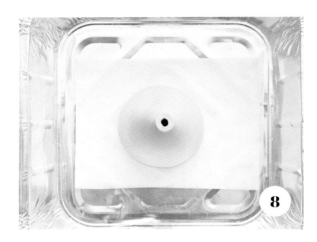

5. Place the cutout cone template on the surface of the clay and cut around it with a craft knife. Cut slowly and move in a line away from your fingers to avoid an accident. Remove the excess clay.

6. Gently lift the clay from underneath the template. Put the paper to one side. Wrap the cone around on itself so the two straight edges come together. Blend the join together on both the inside and outside with your fingers by smoothing over the line with a little pressure.

7. When the join looks seamless, place it on the circle of clay. Be sure the edges are aligned and blend the cone and the circle together with your fingers.

8. Preheat the oven to 230°F (110°C). Line a foil baking tray with an 8 x 8–inch (20 x 20–cm) piece of parchment paper. Carefully transfer the clay to the foil tray and cover it with a second tray. Heat it in the oven for 30 minutes. When the time is up, remove the tray from the oven and leave the clay to cool entirely before lifting it out. To use, pour a reed diffuser oil into the hole in the top of the diffuser and add three or four reeds.

COLOR-BLOCK PHOTO HOLDER

Don't let your treasured memories get lost in the camera roll: Print them out and keep them where you'll always see them. For these abstract photo holders, I've used beautiful neutral colors to add calming accents to side tables, shelves or credenzas. The colors are gently mixed together so they sit side by side without blending together. Combining these colors before cutting the clay gives an abstract pattern to the whole piece, not just the front, which means the piece looks stunning from every direction. This makes the photo holders ideal for areas in your home that are on display.

materials

3.5 oz (100 g) terra-cotta FIMO polymer clay

3.5 oz (100 g) cognac FIMO polymer clay

3.5 oz (100 g) champagne FIMO polymer clay

3.5 oz (100 g) flesh FIMO polymer clay

2 (1 x 15 x 1" [2.5 x 38 x 2.5–cm]) lengths of wood

Roller

2.5" (6-cm) circle cookie cutter

Clay slicer tool

Parchment paper

2 (10 x 10" [25 x 25–cm]) foil baking trays

Medium-grain wet-or-dry sandpaper

Microfiber cloth

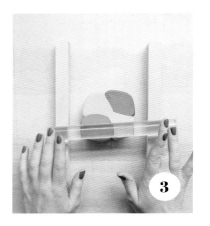

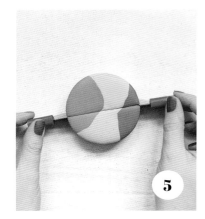

1. Take each color of clay and hold it between your palms to warm it. After 30 seconds, begin to work the clay in your hands. Roll it out, twist it together and ball it back up several times until it is soft and pliable.

2. Ball the clay up into irregular shapes and place them on a nonstick surface. Press the pieces together so they are touching.

3. Place the lengths of wood on either side of the clay and roll the clay out until the roller runs smoothly over the clay and it's an even thickness with the wood. The balls of clay should blend together to give a smooth surface with no change in the surface of the clay apart from the color.

4. Press the cookie cutter into the surface of the clay, using the flat of your hand to apply even pressure. Twist the cutter slightly in both directions to prevent it from sticking to the clay. Lift the cutter out of the outer piece of clay. Gently press the circle of clay left inside the cutter out to one side on the nonstick surface.

5. Using the clay slicer tool, cut the circle in two along the middle. Think about the placement of the colors before you cut; you want to create two pieces that include a mix of all three colors. Place the tool gently on the surface of the clay in position across the circle. Push the slicer down through the clay slowly to keep it straight.

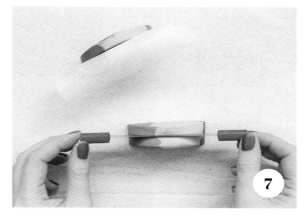

6. Smooth over the edges of the clay with your finger so the edges are rounded. Place the semicircle on the straight edge of a piece of parchment paper.

7. Place the slicer on the top of the dome in the center. Push the slicer down into the clay around 1 inch (2.5 cm) and pull it back up and out again. Slot a small piece of parchment paper inside of this slice, between the two sides of clay, to stop them sticking together while baking.

8. Preheat the oven to 230°F (110°C). Line a foil baking tray with an 8 x 8–inch (20 x 20–cm) piece of parchment paper. Carefully transfer the clay to the foil tray and cover it with a second tray. Heat it in the oven for 30 minutes. When the time is up, remove the tray from the oven and leave the clay to cool entirely before lifting it out.

9. Sometimes small fibers or debris can sit on the surface of the clay. You can gently sand these away, as well as any unexpected lumps and bumps, using sandpaper. Wet the sandpaper with a small amount of water and gently rub over the clay where the imperfection is. Wipe the clay with a damp cloth and dry it with a clean microfiber cloth.

BEDSIDE TABLE CLOCK

Are you always running ten minutes late? This bedside clock will help keep you in check and upgrade your bedroom decor at the same time. Light grey fits seamlessly with any color combination, and this couldn't be simpler to make. You'll use just two layers of clay to build up this stand-alone clock. The minimal design requires accuracy and symmetry, so we're using a handmade template to cut the clay pieces. This makes it super easy to line up the pieces and create a smooth, professional finish.

materials

Cardstock

3.5" (9-cm) circle cookie cutter

Pencil

Ruler

Scissors

8 oz (200 g) dolphin grey FIMO polymer clay

2 (1 x 15 x 0.5" [2.5 x 38 x 1.5–cm]) lengths of wood

Roller

Craft knife

Parchment paper

2.5" (6-cm) circle cookie cutter

Blending tools

Plastic straw

2 (10 x 10" [25 x 25–cm]) foil baking trays

Clock mechanism

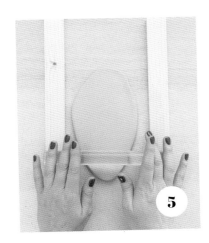

1. Make the clock template from a piece of cardstock: Take the larger cookie cutter and place it 1 inch (2.5 cm) from the bottom edge of your cardstock. Draw around the outside of the cookie cutter using a pencil and place the cookie cutter to one side.

2. With the bottom edge facing toward you, draw two straight lines from the outermost points of the circle down to the edge of the cardstock with a ruler. Measure the distance between these lines along the length to ensure they are an even distance the whole way.

3. Cut around the outside line to create an arch-shape template.

4. Hold the piece of clay between your palms to warm it. After 30 seconds, begin to work the clay in your hands. Roll it out, twist it together and ball it back up several times until it is soft and pliable. When all the clay is warm, bring it together in one ball.

5. Place the clay between the lengths of wood on a nonstick surface. Roll out the clay until the roller runs smoothly over the clay and it's an even thickness with the wood.

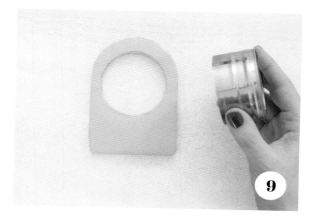

6. Place the template over the clay, gently pressing it into position with your fingers. Use the craft knife to cut the clay, using the outside of the template as a guide. Be sure you cut away from your other hand to avoid accidents. Remove the clay outside of the template area. Carefully lift the template from the clay and the clay from the surface. Place the clay back down on a piece of parchment paper.

7. Ball up the remaining clay and place it between the lengths of wood again. Roll it out and place the template on top of the clay. Cut another piece of clay that should be an exact match to the first arch.

8. Remove the template from the clay. Place the smaller cookie cutter on top of this second piece of clay, keeping it in line with the rounded edge at the top of the piece. Make sure the curve at the top of the cookie cutter is aligned with the curve at the top of the clay arch. The cookie cutter should sit in a central position.

9. Press the cookie cutter into the surface of the clay, using the flat of your hand to apply even pressure. Twist the cutter slightly in both directions to prevent it from sticking to the clay. Lift the cutter out of the outer piece of clay and place it to one side. Hopefully the clay inside of the cookie cutter sticks inside the ring and is removed with it. Don't worry if it doesn't; as you lift the clay in the next step, let the circle of clay stay on the surface.

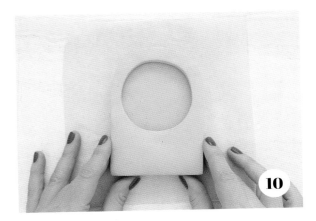

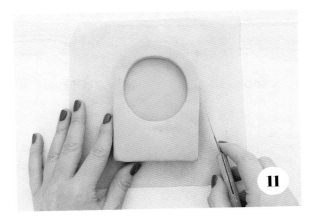

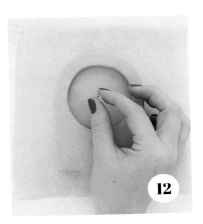

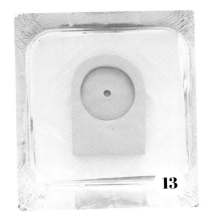

10. Lift the second arch shape; this is the one with the circle cut out from the middle. Place it on top of the first one. The circle will fall out of shape as you transfer the clay. Line up the edges around the arch and gently insert the smaller cookie cutter back into the hole to ensure the shape is a perfect circle.

11. Using your finger or a blending tool, blend the join around the outside of the pieces until it is smooth and seamless. Then, use a large blending tool to ensure the edges are clean.

12. Find the center point of the circle face and push the straw into the clay, creating a hole for the clock parts.

13. Preheat the oven to 230°F (110°C). Transfer the parchment paper and clay to a foil baking tray and cover it with a second tray. Heat it in the oven for 30 minutes. When the time is up, remove the tray from the oven and leave the clay to cool entirely before lifting the clay out.

14. When the clay is cooled, fit the clock mechanism through the hole in the center of the circle face.

CATCHALL TRAY

A catchall tray can be a great way to keep clutter at bay. The trick is to make such a beautiful tray that practically anything you place on it looks amazing! It's a big ask, but I think that this tray is up to the challenge.

The legs give this tray an elevated platform, allowing it to stand alone as a statement piece. One of the big advantages of using air-dry clay is that it works well with adhesives, making life much easier! The plinth-like legs could not be easier to make and we can attach the pieces after drying them.

materials

35 oz (1 kg) white DAS air-dry clay

2 (1 x 15 x 1" [2.5 x 38 x 2.5–cm]) lengths of wood

Roller

2.5" (6-cm) circle cookie cutter

Parchment paper

2 (1 x 15 x 0.5" [2.5 x 38 x 1.5–cm]) lengths of wood

Ruler

Paper

4.25" (11-cm) circle cookie cutter

Pencil

Scissors

Craft knife

Damp sponge

Fine-grain sandpaper

Strong multi-purpose glue

Sponge brush or paint brush

Latex paint

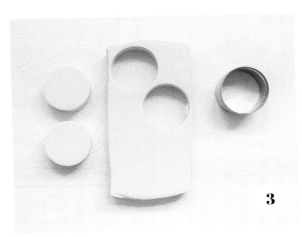

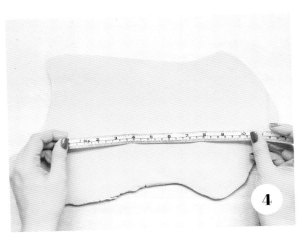

1. Place the clay on a nonstick surface between the two 1-inch (2.5-cm) lengths of wood. Roll out the clay until the roller runs smoothly over the clay and it's an even thickness with the wood.

2. Press the smaller cookie cutter into the surface of the clay, using the flat of your hand to apply even pressure. Twist the cutter slightly in both directions to prevent it from sticking to the clay. Lift the cutter out of the outer piece of clay. Gently press the circle of clay left inside the cutter out to one side on the nonstick surface.

3. Repeat Step 2 again so you have two circles of clay. Place them on a piece of parchment paper, smooth over the surface with water and leave them to dry for 48 hours.

4. Ball up the remaining clay and place it on a nonstick surface between the 0.5-inch (1.5-cm) lengths of wood. Roll out the clay into a long oval roughly 10 x 6 inches (25 x 15 cm).

5. Create a template for the tray shape: Fold a piece of paper in half along the width. Place the larger circle cookie cutter at one end of the fold so that it is half on the paper and half off over the fold.

6. Using a pencil, draw around the outside of the cookie cutter onto the paper. Move the cookie cutter along the fold until the outlines are touching. When you have two semicircles along the fold, draw a line between the peaks of both circles.

7. Cut along the outer line, ignoring all the marks inside. Unfold the paper and run your finger along the fold to flatten.

8. Place the template over the clay, gently pressing it into position with your fingers. Use the craft knife to cut the clay, using the outside of the template as a guide. Cut away from your other hand to avoid accidents. Remove the clay outside of the template area.

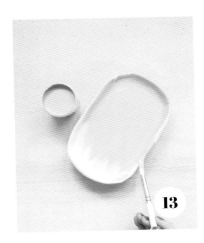

9. Peel back the clay at one end of the oblong and slide your hand underneath. Transfer the clay to a piece of parchment paper. Smooth the clay with a damp sponge, making sure the edges are clean and crisp.

10. Lift the edges up gently with your fingers to create a lip around the edge of the clay.

11. Leave the clay to dry in a warm place for 48 hours. Once it's dry, sand the entire surface with a fine-grain sandpaper, rubbing the surface in small circles until it is smooth and free from bumps or rough areas.

12. Add a generous amount of glue to the top of both circle pieces of clay. Press them onto the bottom of the tray section, positioning one at either end in the center. Leave to dry for 1 hour.

13. Use the sponge brush to paint on two to three thin layers of paint, leaving the paint to dry completely between each layer.

MATISSE-INSPIRED MOBILE

You can have a lot of fun with clay. Sometimes it can be cathartic and healing to let yourself go with the flow and create something without knowing exactly what the final result will look like. So instead of giving you templates or instructions on how to create each shape, I'm going to hand you the creative reins on this project. Experimenting is the best way to learn and find new ideas. This project is about taking that chance to find new shapes, color combinations and compositions with the clay. And at the end, you'll have a piece of art that is unique to you!

I personally love this color combination. It is a nod to the bright palette the artist Matisse often stuck to. His collages have a bold, organic feel to them. Feel free to pick out your favorite colors and personalize this piece to your own tastes. Hang this mobile next to a window and watch the shadows dance as the light hits the moving shapes.

materials

1.75 oz (50 g) gold FIMO polymer clay

2 (1 x 15 x 0.13" [2.5 x 38 x 0.3–cm]) lengths of wood

Roller

Toothpick

Craft knife

Blending tool

2 (10 x 10" [25 x 25–cm]) foil baking trays

Parchment paper

1.75 oz (50 g) windsor blue FIMO polymer clay

1.75 oz (50 g) leaf green FIMO polymer clay

1.75 oz (50 g) terra-cotta FIMO polymer clay

1.75 oz (50 g) blush pink FIMO polymer clay

0.25" (5-mm) round wood dowel

Scissors

Thin cotton cord

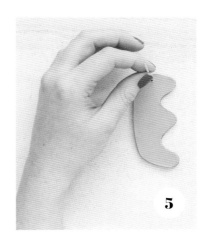

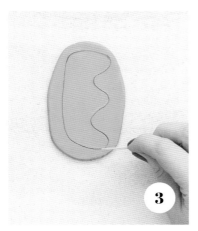

1. Remove half the gold clay from one packet and work it until it is warm and soft, rolling and balling up the clay until it is easy to manipulate.

2. Place the soft clay on a nonstick surface between the lengths of wood. Roll out the clay until the roller runs smoothly over the clay and it's an even thickness with the wood.

3. Using the toothpick, draw out two shapes on the surface of the clay. Take inspiration from Matisse or create your own shapes. Get creative!

4. Cut out the shapes with the craft knife. Cut away from your other hand to avoid accidents. It is sometimes easier to cut roughly around the shape, then go back in and cut around more detailed sections later on. When you are finished, remove the clay outside of the shape.

Smooth around the edges of the shape with a blending tool or your finger. Turn the piece over so you can blend along both sides of the edge.

5. Decide which way your shape will hang and make a hole at the top of the shape in the center with a toothpick.

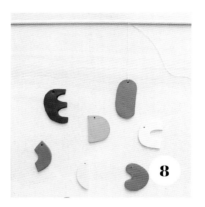

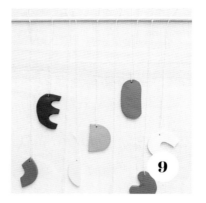

6. Line a foil baking tray with an 8 x 8–inch (20 x 20–cm) piece of parchment paper. Transfer the shapes to the foil tray. Repeat Steps 1 through 6 with the other four packets of clay.

Preheat the oven to 230°F (110°C). When all the shapes are ready, cover the foil tray with a second tray. Heat it in the oven for 30 minutes. When the time is up, remove the tray from the oven and leave the clay to cool entirely before lifting the clay out.

7. Take each piece of clay out and lay it on a flat surface. Start playing with the composition of the pieces as if they were hanging from your mobile.

8. Place the dowel in position on the surface above the clay shapes. Cut off 15 inches (40 cm) of cord and tie one end to the hole in your first clay shape. Tie the other end to the dowel, keeping everything in place and ensuring the cord is pulled tight.

9. Tie each shape to the dowel in the same way. When you're finished, make sure the pieces all hang as you imagined. Make any adjustments by cutting the cord and tying again.

10. Cut a 20-inch (50-cm) piece of cord. Tie one end of the cord to one end of the dowel and the other end of the cord to the other end of the dowel. Attach a screw in or an adhesive hook to the ceiling and hang your piece in place.

CORDLESS WALL LAMP

Did you know you're meant to have seven sources of light in every room? For smaller spaces, that might seem a little extreme, but it just goes to show you can never have enough lamps. The problem is finding enough space for all these light sources, especially in smaller spaces such as the bedroom. I've come up with a small solution to this problem with this cordless wall lamp. This light bulb is power cord–free, allowing you to place the light anywhere without being restricted by available power sockets. The LED light stays cool to minimize risk of overheating, but for safety reasons don't leave the light on unattended.

materials

10.5 oz (300 g) flesh FIMO air-dry clay

1 tsp ground black pepper

2 (1 x 15 x 1" [2.5 x 38 x 2.5–cm]) lengths of wood

Roller

3" (7.5-cm) circle cookie cutter

Craft knife

Parchment paper

Damp sponge

Small wood blending tool

LED pull-cord, battery-operated lightbulb

Fine-grain sandpaper

Microfiber cloth

Heavy-duty adhesive strip

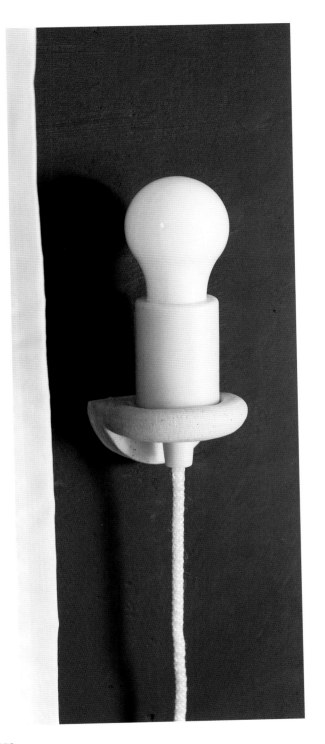

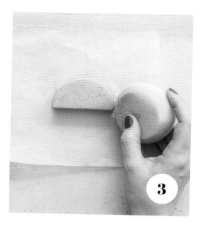

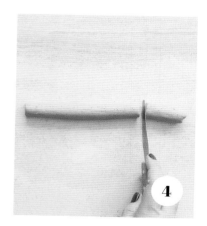

1. Take 9 ounces (250 g) of clay out of the packet. Sprinkle the black pepper over the clay and work it in, kneading and rolling the clay until the pepper is evenly spread throughout. Place the clay on a nonstick surface between the two lengths of wood. Roll out the clay until the roller runs smoothly over the clay and it's an even thickness with the wood.

2. Press the cookie cutter into the surface of the clay, using the flat of your hand to apply even pressure. Twist the cutter slightly in both directions to prevent it from sticking to the clay. Lift the cutter out of the outer piece of clay. Gently press the circle of clay left inside the cutter out to one side on the nonstick surface.

3. Cut the circle in half using a craft knife. Put one half of the clay to the side; you can make a second lamp with this piece. Transfer the clay to a piece of parchment paper and smooth over the surface of the clay with a damp sponge.

4. Take the leftover clay and add the remaining 1.5 ounces (50 g) from the packet. Roll it into a tube shape about 0.5 inch (1.5 cm) thick. Cut it into a piece 6 inches (15 cm) long.

5. Score both ends of the tube and corners of your semicircle piece of clay with a craft knife. Try to score a small circle the ends of the tube will cover.

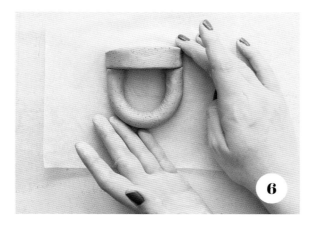

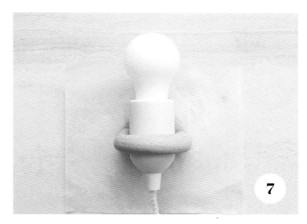

6. With the piece of parchment paper to help you, lift the semicircle piece of clay so it is sitting on its straight edge. Press one end of the tube onto one scored corner. Press the other end of the tube into the second scored corner and blend both the joins with a small wood blending tool, moving the clay over the join to create a seamless connection.

7. Be sure your clay tube is creating a rounded, symmetrical shape that is big enough for your light to fit inside.

8. Leave the clay for 48 hours to dry and harden. When the clay is ready, sand the surface, rubbing the fine-grain sandpaper from side to side to create a clean, smooth surface. Wipe off the debris with a damp cloth.

9. Use a heavy-duty adhesive strip to attach the fixture to the wall. Thread the cord from the light bulb into the center of the clay and rest the bulb on the top. When you want to switch the lamp on and off, just hold the bulb and pull the cord.

TOTAL ECLIPSE MOON BANNER

This banner is such a great addition to a picture gallery wall, or you can hang it on its own as a focal piece. Try it horizontally across the wall over a headboard, or use it vertically in a small space that's difficult to decorate.

This project uses a more free-form technique to create an organic line between colors in the clay. To achieve the best results, be sure the transition between the lines is smooth and seamless without blending them together. Your roller will do all the work. Give yourself a thick base of clay to start with; the more you have to roll, the better the clay will come together.

materials

9 oz (250 g) white DAS air-dry clay

2 (1 x 15 x 0.25" [2.5 x 38 x 0.6–cm]) lengths of wood

Roller

3.5 oz (100 g) terra-cotta air-dry clay

2.5" (6-cm) circle cookie cutter

Toothpick

Parchment paper

Fine-grain sandpaper

Microfiber cloth

Sponge brush or paint brush

Polyurethane water-based varnish

Scissors

Cotton cord

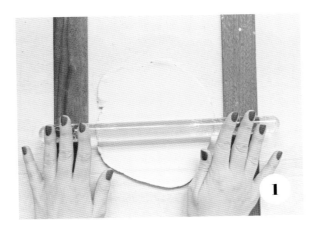

1. Place the white clay on a nonstick surface between the two lengths of wood. Roll out the clay until the roller runs smoothly over the clay and it's an even thickness with the wood.

2. Weigh out 2.5 ounces (70 g) of terra-cotta clay and roll it into a ball between your palms. Once it is in a ball shape, squeeze it between your palms to flatten slightly.

3. Place the terra-cotta clay in the center of the rolled-out white clay. Place the roller back over the clay and wood and roll over the terra-cotta clay until it sits in the middle of the white clay with a seamless join.

4. Now it's time to cut out the circles for the different moon phases. Place the cookie cutter on the surface of the clay so the clay inside is mostly terra-cotta. Next are two half-moon phases. Cut these from half the terra-cotta and half the white clay. Finally, the last two will be all white for the full moon. Use the clay outside the terra-cotta circle to create these. You might need to cut off the white clay, roll it into a ball and roll it out again to make the two circles from white clay. Press the cookie cutter into the surface of the clay, using the flat of your hand to apply even pressure. Twist the cutter slightly in both directions to prevent it from sticking to the clay. Lift the cutter out of the outer piece of clay. Gently press the circle of clay left inside the cutter out to one side on the nonstick surface.

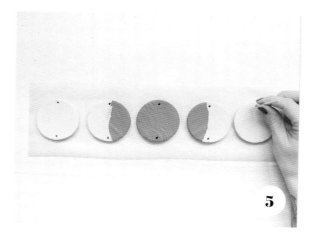

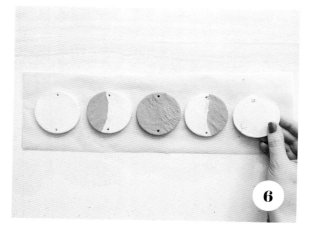

5. Use a toothpick to create a hole in the top and bottom of the crescent moon, the half-moon shapes and one of the full moon shapes. In the other full moon, make just one hole close to the edge. Gently twist the toothpick into the clay to create the hole. Once through, twist it back out, then push the toothpick through the hole on the opposite side of the clay to neaten it up.

6. Place each piece of clay on a piece of parchment paper and leave them to dry for 24 to 48 hours. Turn the clay over every 12 hours.

7. When the clay is hard, rub a fine-grain sandpaper over the edges, using your hands to hold the sandpaper. Run it along the edge to create a clean line. Wipe off the debris with a damp cloth.

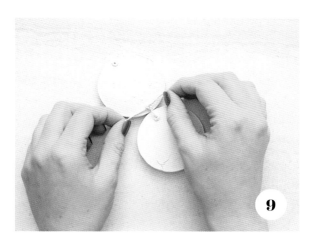

8. Use a sponge brush to apply two light layers of varnish. Make sure the first layer dries fully before applying the second coat.

9. Cut 3-inch (8-cm) pieces of cord. Tie them to the holes in the clay, connecting the moon phases together starting with a full moon to half-moon to crescent moon to half-moon to full moon.

10. Tie a final piece of cord to the remaining hole in the full moon. At the other end of the cord, tie a loop to allow the piece to hang from a nail or hook.

bathroom

You might not immediately think of using clay in the bathroom, but it's a fantastic material to experiment with in this area. Polymer clay is completely waterproof, which makes it ideal for a wet environment, but don't let the humidity stop you from using air-dry clay in this room too. A good varnish will protect your clay from moisture in the air, allowing you to use air-dry clay without fear for projects such as the Terra-Cotta Jewelry Dish (page 134).

It's also a great place to inject some personality. Bathroom decor can be braver without fear of the results. It's a small room with an enormous impact! Use these projects as a way to try new things and push your design boundaries. The Wave Soap Dish (page 130) uses a beautiful marbled polymer clay slab. Each one is totally unique, and you never know how the pattern will work out. The effect is easy to achieve with a few twists of the clay. You'll be creating marbled everything once you've tried this!

WAVE SOAP DISH

More and more of us are making the switch from liquid to bar soap for environmental reasons. This gives us a fantastic opportunity to add in a little detail and color around the sink. A soap dish, while not a necessity, makes for a much nicer experience for you and your guests when trying to keep your hands clean.

Polymer clay is the perfect material for creating your soap dishes. It is easy to clean and waterproof, and it can be molded into some fun shapes! I'm using a simple technique to create the shape of this dish: The trick to keeping the curves neat and uniform is using small round wood dowels to keep the clay in place as it is heated and sets.

materials

2 oz (60 g) translucent FIMO polymer clay	2 (1 x 15 x 0.25" [2.5 x 38 x 0.6–cm]) lengths of wood
0.5 oz (15 g) champagne FIMO polymer clay	Roller
	Ruler
0.35 oz (10 g) pink FIMO polymer clay	Craft knife
	Parchment paper
0.1 oz (3 g) terra-cotta FIMO polymer clay	2 (10 x 10" [25 x 25–cm]) foil baking trays
3.5 oz (100 g) white FIMO polymer clay	8 (0.25" [0.6-cm]) round wood dowels

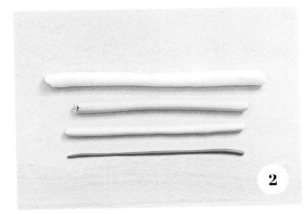

1. Measure out 1 ounce (30 g) of the translucent clay and hold the clay between your palms to warm it. After 30 seconds, begin to work the clay in your hands. Roll it out, twist it together and ball it back up several times until it is soft and pliable. Warm and work all of the champagne clay, the pink clay and the terracotta clay the same way.

2. Roll out each color of clay into a solid tube shape. Start by placing your fingertips on the clay. Push your hands forward, rolling the clay underneath them on the work surface until you reach the bottom of your palms. Then bring your hands back toward you, never losing contact with the clay.

3. Twist all the pieces of clay together into one piece of clay and roll it underneath your hands again.

4. After 10 seconds, fold the tube in half and roll it into a ball. Roll it into a tube again and repeat the twist.

5. Put this to one side and warm the white clay and the remaining translucent clay. Roll these into tubes. Lay all three pieces of clay next to each other and twist together, then roll it into a ball. Roll it out into a tube, twist and ball up one more time. The clay should have started to mix, but you should still have visible lines of each clay running through. This should give you a very faint marble effect.

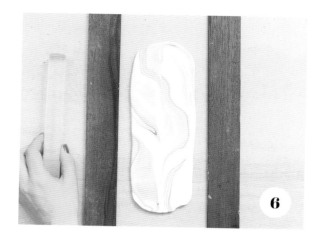

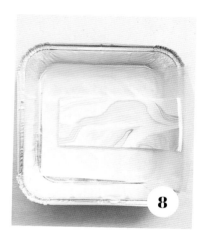

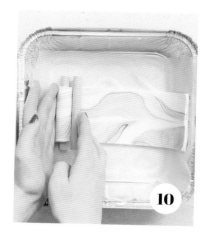

6. Place the clay on a nonstick surface between the lengths of wood. Roll out the clay until the roller runs smoothly over the clay and it's an even thickness with the wood.

7. Measure out a piece from the center of the clay that is 8 x 3 inches (20 x 8 cm). Place the ruler along the measurements and use it to guide the craft knife when cutting the clay. When you've finished slicing, remove the clay from outside the rectangle.

8. Carefully lift the clay off the surface and place it on a piece of parchment paper inside a foil baking tray—this will save you from transferring later.

9. Gently lift one of the shorter ends of the clay and slide a wood dowel underneath. Position the clay so that the very edge is facedown against the bottom of the foil tray, creating an arch over the dowel.

10. Place the next dowel on top of the clay next to the first one. Be sure the dowels sit snuggly against each other and the clay does not look or feel loose in between them.

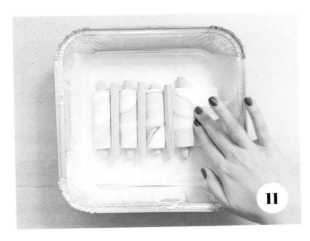

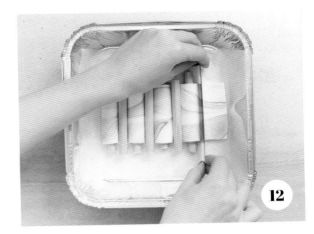

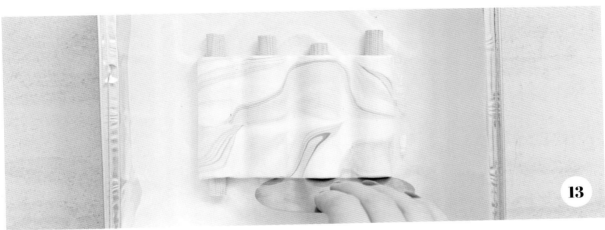

11. Lift the remaining portion of clay and slide in another dowel. Position this one next to the second dowel in the same way, ensuring the clay is wrapped tightly around the dowels. You should start to see the wave pattern beginning to form now.

Continue to place the dowels over and under the clay along the remaining section. You will have three dowels over the top of the clay and four underneath.

12. When you reach the last dowel, position the clay so that the shorter edge is facing down on the foil tray, mirroring the opposite side.

You might need to cut off small sections of clay to do this. Remove the last dowel. With a ruler and craft knife, slice off a small slice from the end of the clay and insert the dowel again. Repeat until your clay folds down over the dowel and touches the tray.

13. Preheat the oven to 230°F (110°C). Cover the foil tray with a second tray. Heat it in the oven for 30 minutes. When the time is up, remove the tray from the oven and leave the clay to cool entirely before lifting the clay out.

TERRA-COTTA JEWELRY DISH

How I love a jewelry dish! They are perfect for collecting and keeping safe all manner of small trinkets and objects. Keeping a stylish jewelry dish in your bathroom keeps your rings, necklaces and earrings safe when you remove them. It's the perfect place to leave two or three pieces of jewelry so that they are easy to grab when you're in a rush.

Here we combine three techniques—using molds, cutting the clay and building—to create the clean look of this jewelry dish. Joining and smoothing is an important step in bringing these processes together. Take your time to achieve a smooth transition between pieces. While we're talking about smooth transitions, don't skip the sanding step, especially in the bowl.

materials

35 oz (1 kg) terra-cotta DAS air-dry clay

2 (1 x 15 x 1" [2.5 x 38 x 2.5–cm]) lengths of wood

Roller

2" (5-cm) circle cookie cutter

4" (10-cm) plastic funnel

Baby oil

Wire clay carving tool

3.5" (9-cm) circle cookie cutter

Parchment paper

Damp sponge

Clay slicer tool

Medium-grain sandpaper

Fine-grain sandpaper

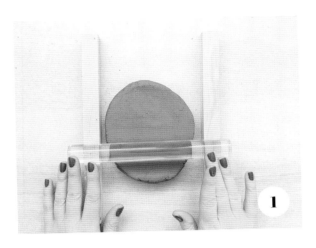

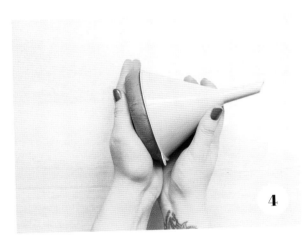

1. Take 17.5 ounces (500 g) of clay out of the packet. Place the clay on a nonstick surface between the two lengths of wood. Roll out the clay until the roller runs smoothly over the clay and it's an even thickness with the wood.

2. Press the smaller cookie cutter into the surface of the clay, using the flat of your hand to apply even pressure. Twist the cutter slightly in both directions to prevent it from sticking to the clay. Lift the cutter out of the outer piece of clay. Gently press the circle of clay left inside the cutter out to one side on the nonstick surface.

3. Take the remaining clay and the remaining 17.5 ounces (500 g) from the packet and roll it up into a ball.

4. Coat the inside of the funnel with a layer of baby oil. Place the clay ball in the funnel and, using your fingers, push down so the clay fills the bowl and the top is flat. Cut off the extra clay with a wire clay carving tool.

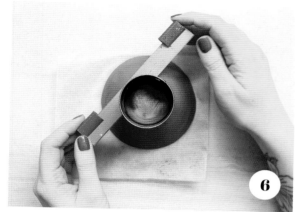

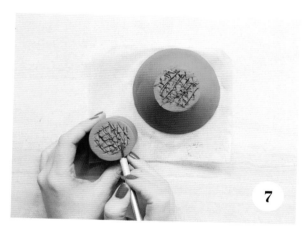

5. Press the larger cookie cutter into the center of the clay in the funnel. Push down evenly about 0.5 inch (1.5 cm). Remove the cookie cutter. Using a wire clay carving tool, start to carve out the clay inside this circle. Carve down to about 0.5 inch (1.5 cm). Create a smooth, flat bottom to the dish.

6. Turn the clay out of the funnel onto a piece of parchment paper and smooth over the surface of the clay with a damp sponge. Place the smaller cookie cutter on the pointy end of the funnel. Press down so that the bottom of the cutter meets the clay. Use a clay slicer tool to cut across the funnel at this point.

7. Score the clay where you've just cut it and on the top of the circle you put to one side earlier. Place the clay circle on the funnel, putting the scored sides together. Blend the join together. Smooth the clay from one side of the join to the other in opposite directions with your fingers. Use a little water to help. Leave this to dry for 48 to 72 hours.

8. Sand the entire surface of both pieces of clay. Start with the medium-grain sandpaper, gently rubbing it over the surface in small circles. Brush away the powdered clay that remains. Sand again with a fine-grain sandpaper to create a smooth surface texture.

CURL-UP INCENSE HOLDER

During the colder months, incense is my go-to for creating a calming, warm feeling in my home. Scent plays such a huge part in our emotional well-being and it's often overlooked. Even just the routine of lighting and extinguishing the flame can help you to relax and get into the right frame of mind.

The building technique in this project creates a fun statement piece that will put a smile on your face no matter how your day is going.

materials

3.5 oz (100 g) champagne FIMO polymer clay

Clay knife carving tool

Parchment paper

2 (10 x 10" [25 x 25–cm]) foil baking trays

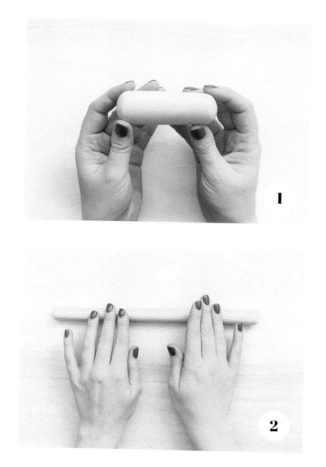

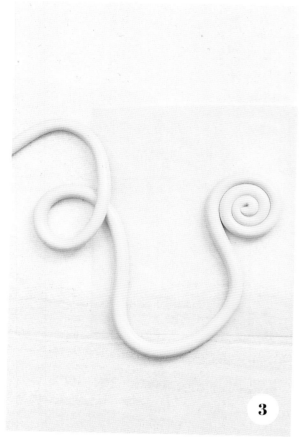

1. Cut the clay into four pieces and warm each one in your hands, rolling and balling up the clay until it is soft and easy to manipulate. When all the clay is soft, bring it back together into a ball. Squeeze the clay into a slightly rounded shape to make it easier to roll.

2. Place the clay on a large nonstick surface so you are looking at it horizontally. Roll out the clay into a solid tube shape. Start by placing your fingertips on the clay. Push your hands forward, rolling the clay underneath them on the surface until you reach the bottom of your palms. Then bring your hands back toward you, never losing contact with the clay.

Continue this action, moving your hands along the entire length of the tube to create an even pressure as you roll. This should help you create an even shape. This might take some practice to get perfect; remember, you can easily ball up the clay and start again.

3. Keep rolling out the clay until you have a piece that is 34 inches (85 cm) in length and about 0.5 inch (1.5 cm) thick. Cut the end to give a clean line. Turn the end of the clay into a tight coil and place it on a piece of parchment paper.

Continue wrapping the clay around itself into a flat coil until the piece reaches 3 inches (7 cm) in diameter.

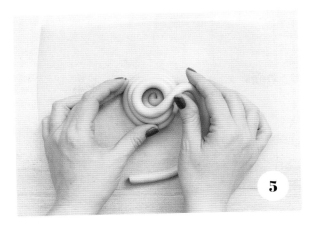

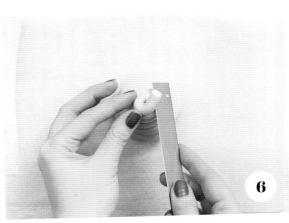

4. Bring the remaining tube of clay up and over the top of the coil. Run the clay along the line between the two outer rings of clay.

5. When you meet the start of the clay in your coil, move the clay up and over the first coil, running the next circle of clay slightly inside to create another loop. Make sure the clay is still touching the last loop at all times.

6. Follow the line of clay, ensuring you lay the clay slightly inside the last circle. This will make a cone shape. When the cone meets at the top, cut off the excess and wrap it into place.

7. Preheat the oven to 230°F (110°C). Carefully transfer the holder and parchment paper to a foil baking tray and cover it with a second tray. Heat it in the oven for 30 minutes. When the time is up, remove the tray from the oven and leave the clay to cool entirely before lifting it out.

SPECKLED HOOP WALL HOOK

When I said you could never have enough hooks in your house, I meant it! These bathroom hooks are larger for towels, robes and just generally looking fabulous. I'm using a different speckling technique than we've previously used. The dark speckle sits in high contrast with the lighter base.

The key to creating small enough pieces for your dark speckle from baked polymer clay is grating. The hard polymer clay grates into much smaller pieces than when soft. I use a nutmeg grater, as this breaks the clay up into chunks rather than slices.

materials

2 (10 x 10" [25 x 25–cm]) foil baking trays

Parchment paper

0.35 oz (10 g) black FIMO polymer clay

5 oz (150 g) soft grey FIMO polymer clay

2 (1 x 15 x 0.75" [2.5 x 38 x 2–cm]) lengths of wood

Roller

Fine grater

Small blender or immersion blender

4" (10-cm) circle cookie cutter

2.5" (6-cm) circle cookie cutter

Plastic straw

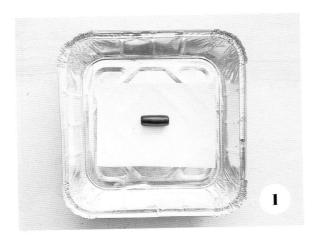

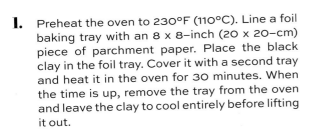

1. Preheat the oven to 230°F (110°C). Line a foil baking tray with an 8 x 8–inch (20 x 20–cm) piece of parchment paper. Place the black clay in the foil tray. Cover it with a second tray and heat it in the oven for 30 minutes. When the time is up, remove the tray from the oven and leave the clay to cool entirely before lifting it out.

2. While the black clay is baking, break the grey clay into four pieces and warm each piece between your palms. After around 30 seconds, start rolling a piece into a tube, then back into a ball several times until the clay feels soft and malleable. When it does, add the next piece of clay and continue to repeat the process until all the clay is in one ball.

3. Place the soft clay on a nonstick surface and place the lengths of wood on either side. Roll out the clay until the roller runs smoothly over both the clay and the wood, creating an even thickness throughout the clay. Lift the clay off the surface and onto a piece of parchment paper.

4. Once the baked black clay has cooled, grate it onto a sheet of parchment paper, then transfer the grated clay into a blender. I use a separate cup on my blender for all things crafty. Pulse the clay once or twice to create a grainy consistency.

5. From a height of around 12 inches (30 cm), sprinkle the finely ground black clay over the surface of the grey clay to give a random, speckled effect.

6. Press the larger cookie cutter into the surface of the clay, using the flat of your hand to apply even pressure. Twist the cutter slightly in both directions to prevent it from sticking to the clay. Lift the cutter out of the outer piece of clay. Gently press the circle of clay left inside the cutter out onto a piece of parchment paper.

7

9

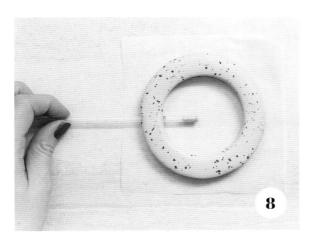

8

7. Place the smaller cookie cutter in the center of the piece of clay. It's worth taking time to find the correct placement in the middle of the outer circle, as this will help to ensure the hook is evenly sized around the entire circle. Press the cookie cutter into the clay, twist a little in both directions and remove the cutter and circle of clay.

8. Place the end of the straw in the middle of the edge of the circle. Push it through the clay and into the center, twisting as you go to ease the straw through. You will use this hole to attach the hook to the wall. It doesn't matter where on the circle it is, but if there's a particular part of the pattern you like, then you can make it more prominent by positioning the hole so that pattern is at the front of the ring.

9. Preheat the oven to 230°F (110°C). Transfer the parchment paper and clay to a foil tray. Cover it with a second tray and heat it in the oven for 30 minutes. When the time is up, remove the tray from the oven and leave the clay to cool entirely before lifting it out. To hang the hook, drill a hole in the wall and insert the appropriate anchor plug. Push a long screw into the hole from the center of the circle and screw into the anchor plug.

FLUTED LIGHT PULL

You'll never look at your light pulls in the same way again. Once you realize how easy it is to make your own, you'll be hooked! And while there's no limit to your creativity, this project uses a stamp to create a pattern. I hope it shows how you can think outside the box when it comes to creating patterns in your clay pieces. Here I've used the edge of a metal scraper tool, but a credit card, the flat edge of a butter knife, a stiff piece of card or even a piece of string pulled tight would achieve the same result. Sometimes just looking around at what you have can spark inspiration.

materials

1 oz (30 g) terra-cotta FIMO polymer clay

2 (1 x 15 x 0.25" [2.5 x 38 x 0.6–cm]) lengths of wood

Roller

Cone template:

- Top diameter: 0.25" (5 mm)
- Bottom diameter: 1.5" (4 cm)
- Height: 2.5" (6 cm)

Craft knife

Parchment paper

Credit card or metal scraper tool

Blending tool

Toothpick

2 (10 x 10" [25 x 25–cm]) foil baking trays

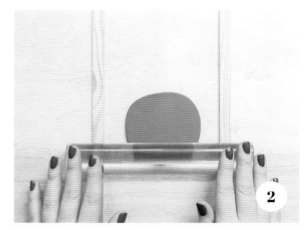

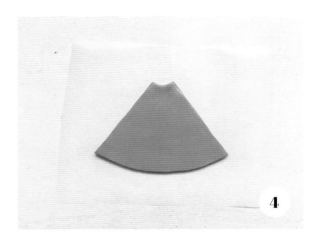

1. Hold the clay between your palms to warm it. After 30 seconds, begin to work the clay in your hands. Roll it out, twist it together and ball it back up several times until it is soft and pliable.

2. Place the clay on a nonstick surface between the lengths of wood. Roll out the clay until the roller runs smoothly over the clay and it's an even thickness with the wood.

3. Place the template over the clay, gently pressing it into position with your fingers. Use the craft knife to cut the clay, using the outside of the template as a guide. Cut away from your other hand to avoid accidents. Remove the clay outside of the template area.

4. Peel back the template and smooth over the edges of the clay. Lift the piece off the surface and onto a piece of parchment paper.

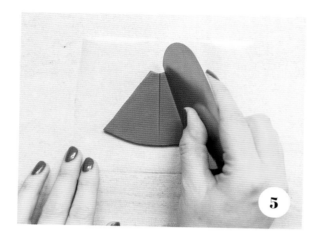

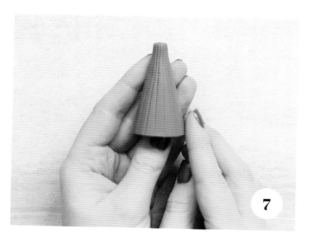

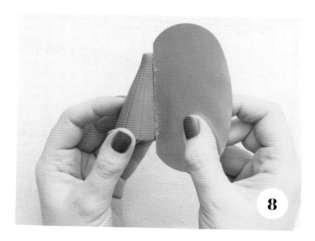

5. Use the side of the credit card or metal scraper tool to create lines along the length of the cone. Start from the center, placing the edge of the card along the center line. Gently push the card into the clay. Remove the card and repeat the process slightly to the right of your first line. As you move your card across the cone, fan out the lines by moving the end of the card closest to you out a little more than the end farthest away from you. You want to create a gradual change in angle along the lines so that your final line is at the same angle as the edge of your clay.

6. Once one side of the clay is complete, work along the opposite side until the whole piece has a patterned texture.

7. Lift the clay off the parchment paper. Using your fingers, gently wrap it around into a cone so that the two straight edges line up. Apply a little pressure to bring them together.

8. Use a small blending tool to gently smooth the clay together over the join in the two pieces of clay. Move the clay in both directions over the join to create a seamless area. Use the credit card to create lines over the join so that there is no break in the pattern.

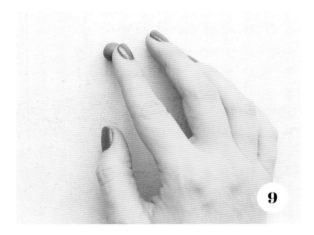

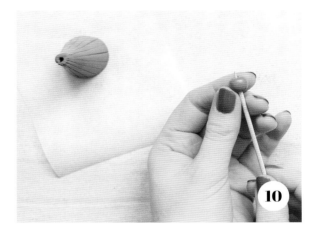

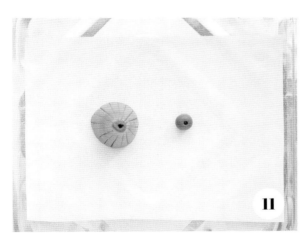

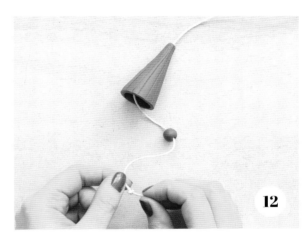

9. Using your fingertips, roll the remaining clay into a ball on a hard surface by gently rolling the clay in circles.

10. Using a toothpick, make a hole in the bead by gently twisting the toothpick through the cooled clay. If the clay is too soft or you push too hard, the bead will squeeze out of shape. When the toothpick reaches the other side of the bead, twist it back out and go back through in the opposite direction. This will ensure the hole is smooth and uniform throughout.

11. Preheat the oven to 230°F (110°C). Carefully transfer the clay and parchment paper to a foil baking tray and cover it with a second tray. Heat it in the oven for 30 minutes. When the time is up, remove the tray from the oven and leave the clay to cool entirely before lifting it out.

12. Thread the cord from your light through the cone first and then through the bead. Tie a knot in the end of the cord underneath the bead and let them hang.

kitchen

There are endless ways to get creative with clay in the kitchen. Handmade items give the kitchen a more lived-in feeling. It's more comforting than a uniform, sterile place. Adding elements of imperfection among the perfectly stacked plates and cups breaks up the monotony. It adds personality and makes it a much more appealing space to be in.

Polymer clay can be submerged in water and cleaned easily. Use food-safe varnishes if you'd like to use the items with food regularly. These are readily available. I use Decopatch Aquapro, which is a food-safe gloss.

This final section of the book gives us a little more scope for imagination and expression. The Salt-and-Pepper Pinch Pot (page 160) gives us the opportunity to work the clay with our hands alone, crafting a small pot from just pushing and pulling the clay into shape. There are also a few new techniques to explore: Slab-making is a stunning way of building up pattern with polymer clay. It's also a terrific way to use offcuts and leftover clay. I'm showing you two different creative uses for a clay slab in this chapter. Both use different techniques to create the surface pattern.

ARCHING COASTER

Every now and then a design trend comes along that is just so fun and aesthetically pleasing it's difficult not to love! The arch or rainbow design is one of those. It's an easy look to create with clean, smooth lines and a satisfying curve. This pale, neutral pink adds to the playful style and complements a range of decorative tastes. These coasters would look just as beautiful on a modern marble breakfast bar as they would on a Scandinavian light-wood coffee table.

Here, I've taken the traditional coaster and given it a modern makeover. Polymer clay stands up to the heat well, and using an extruder creates even arches. The techniques are achievable for even a complete beginner to polymer clay. I use a hobby clay extruder to ensure the tubes are evenly formed. If you don't have access to this tool, you can still create these coasters: Just take care to roll the clay evenly before constructing the arches.

materials

8 oz (200 g) antique rose FIMO polymer clay

Clay knife

Clay extruder

2 (10 x 10" [25 x 25–cm]) foil baking trays

Parchment paper

Fine-grain wet-or-dry sandpaper

Microfiber cloths

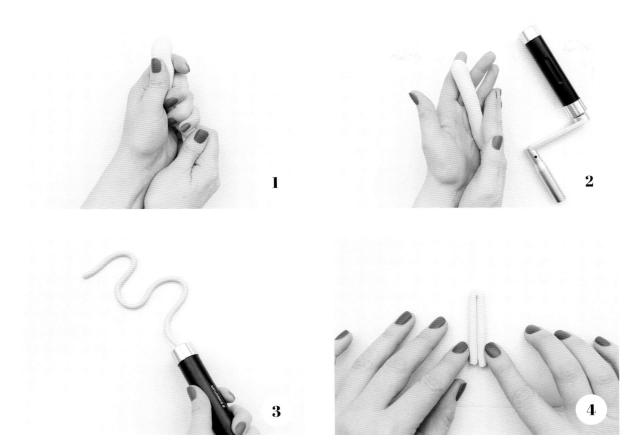

1. Roll, squeeze and stretch the clay repeatedly until it's soft and warm.

2. Cut off about a quarter of the clay and roll it into a rough tube shape about the same size as the extruder tube. Push this into the clay extruder. If you don't have an extruder, roll the clay into a thinner tube to create the arches. You'll need to take your time rolling sections around 12 inches (30 cm) at a time. Move your hands along the tube as you roll to keep the thickness even.

3. If you're using the extruder, follow the extruder instructions to insert the circle extruder part and push the clay out to make the thin tubes. If your clay is warm and pliable, it should come out in a smooth tube. If the clay is cracked, remove it from the extruder and work it in your hands again as described in Step 1.

4. Once you have the tube ready, it's time to make the inner arc. Gently fold the clay onto itself around 1 inch (2.5 cm) from one end, gently pressing the two sides together without distorting the shape. Cut off the longer length of clay where it meets the beginning. Line a foil baking tray with an 8 x 8–inch (20 x 20–cm) piece of parchment paper and place the clay on it.

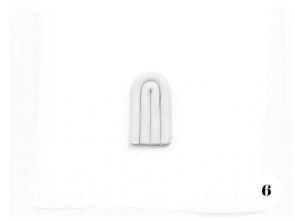

5. Line up one end of the remaining clay tube with the beginning of this first arch. Run the tube over the arch to the other end, gently pressing into place, then cut off the excess (again in line with the straight edge of the arch).

6. Repeat this step seven times to build up the coaster. The lengths of clay will need to be longer each time. To save from wasting the clay, you will need to make more clay tubes using the offcuts.

7. When the arch coaster is complete, use a clay knife to cut the bottom edge straight.

8. Preheat the oven to 230°F (110°C). Cover the foil baking tray with a second tray and heat it in the oven for 30 minutes. When the time is up, remove the tray from the oven and leave the clay to cool entirely before lifting the clay out.

9. Sometimes small fibers or debris can sit on the surface of the clay. You can gently sand these away, as well as any unexpected lumps and bumps, using sandpaper. Wet the sandpaper with a small amount of water and gently rub over the clay where the imperfection is. Wipe over the clay with a damp cloth and dry with a clean microfiber cloth.

STONE-EFFECT SPOON HOLDER

I don't know about you, but a spoon holder is the new addition to our home that I never knew I needed. I've become obsessed. Once you've experienced the delights of a clean work surface, rather than one with pools of sauce dotted over your kitchen surfaces, you'll never go back. And you'll make sure no one else in your home does either!

Many of the projects in this book have a more modern approach to design. This spoon holder focuses more on the traditional effects in the clay. I'm using some techniques to mimic the look of a more classic piece of pottery and adding a little extra texture with the coarsely ground pepper. Sealing the clay with food-safe varnish makes it look like a piece from the kiln and it is perfectly safe to use in your kitchen!

materials

3.5 oz (100 g) white FIMO polymer clay

2 (1 x 15 x 0.25" [2.5 x 38 x 0.6–cm]) lengths of wood

Roller

Parchment paper

1 oz (30 g) champagne FIMO polymer clay

1 tsp ground black pepper

2 (10 x 10" [25 x 25–cm]) foil baking trays

Sponge brush or paint brush

Food-safe varnish, such as Decopatch Aquapro

1. Warm the white clay between your palms and start rolling it into a tube, then back into a ball several times until the clay feels soft and malleable.

2. Place the soft clay on a nonstick surface between the lengths of wood. Roll out the clay, turning the clay regularly to create a rough circle. Keep rolling until the roller runs smoothly over the clay and it's an even thickness with the wood. Carefully transfer it to a piece of parchment paper.

3. Soften the champagne clay and roll it into a ball. Place the ball of clay into the center of the white clay. Roll it again, turning the clay to create an even circle.

4. Sprinkle pepper onto the surface of the clay and gently push the roller over the surface.

5. With your fingers over the top of the clay and your thumbs applying pressure underneath, start gently lifting the edge of the clay into a small lip. Move around the circumference of the circle, lifting and pushing the clay into place as you go.

6. Stop lifting the clay when your lip reaches 2 inches (5 cm) before the start of the lip.

7. Carefully transfer the parchment paper to a foil baking tray. Scrunch up a second piece of parchment paper into a long tube shape. Lift the parchment paper from underneath the clay and place the scrunched-up paper underneath to support the lip. Push it against the clay lip to hold it in place.

8. Preheat the oven to 230°F (110°C). Cover the foil tray with a second tray and heat it in the oven for 30 minutes. When the time is up, remove the tray from the oven and leave the clay to cool entirely before lifting the clay out.

9. Use the sponge brush to spread three light layers of varnish over the surface, leaving each layer for 5 hours to fully dry. Hand-wash the spoon holder as necessary. Dry immediately after washing.

Water plants

Garden Picnic
Movie Night

COOKIE CUTTER FRIDGE MAGNETS

This is a play on the classic alphabet magnets we all had and loved as children—but with a more sophisticated edge. Pin your notes, photos and kids' drawings to the fridge with the most stylish of magnets.

Get ready, because you're about to become addicted to this technique. Slab-making is an incredibly satisfying way to add pattern to your clay. Take care to keep the top, patterned layer of the clay thin; we don't want this to obscure out of shape when we're rolling it into the base clay. Keeping the top layer thin will stop the clay from spreading too far from its original shape.

I use a fondant cutting set to make the shapes; you can find these at craft supply and specialty baking stores. You can cut the floral elements by hand with a craft knife, but this will take more time, especially when working on a larger scale.

materials

8 oz (200 g) white FIMO polymer clay

2 (1 x 15 x 0.25" [2.5 x 38 x 0.6–cm]) lengths of wood

Roller

1.75 oz (50 g) terra-cotta FIMO polymer clay

Parchment paper

0.75" (2-cm) fondant floral plunge cutter

Craft knife

Alphabet cookie cutters

Small circle magnets

2 (10 x 10" [25 x 25–cm]) foil baking trays

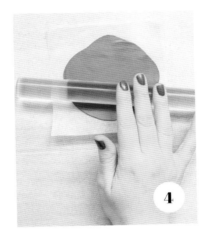

1. Break the white clay into four pieces and warm each one in your hands, rolling and balling up the clay until it is soft and easy to manipulate. When all the clay is soft, bring it back together into a ball.

2. Place the soft clay on a nonstick surface between the lengths of wood. Roll out the clay until the roller runs smoothly over the clay and it's an even thickness with the wood.

3. Hold the terra-cotta clay between your palms to warm it. After 30 seconds, begin to work the clay in your hands. Roll it out, twist it together and ball it back up several times until it is soft and pliable.

4. Place this on a piece of parchment paper and, without using any lengths of wood, roll the clay out thinly.

5. Place the plunge cutter on top of the clay and firmly press down with the palm of your hands. Lift the cutter. If the clay has come away from the paper and is still in the cutter, press the plunger down again to release it. Place the flower back down on a nonstick surface.

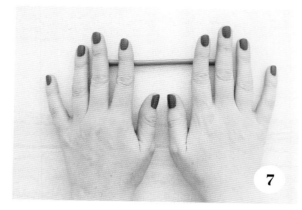

6. Using the craft knife, cut each of the petals off the flower to create leaves. Carefully cut a very shallow line down the center of each leaf. Repeat this process another eight times and place the leaves to one side.

7. Ball up the remaining clay and weigh out 0.35 ounces (10 g). Place the clay on a nonstick surface. Roll out the clay into a solid tube shape. Start by placing your fingertips on the clay. Push your hands forward, rolling the clay underneath them on the surface until you reach the bottom of your palms. Then bring your hands back toward you, never losing contact with the clay.

8. Continue this action, moving your hands along the entire length of the tube to create an even pressure as you roll. This should help you create an even shape. When you have a long, thin piece of clay, you are ready to start building your block. This might take some practice to get perfect; remember, you can easily ball up the clay and start again.

9. Cut the clay into pieces around 3 to 4 inches (7 to 10 cm) long and lay them down vertically along the white clay. You want to create an organic line, so allow the clay to weave left and right as you place it down. Cut off any excess at the top and bottom of the line.

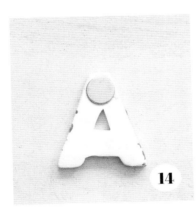

10. Take the leaves and place them along the line as if it were a plant or vine. Place the leaves in a random order to create a natural look. Gently press the leaves into place with your fingers.

11. Keep building up the pattern over the surface of the clay until it is filled. Cover the clay with a piece of parchment paper and press it down in between the leaves and lines with your fingertips.

12. Place your roller gently on top of the parchment paper and roll along the clay, adding a very small amount of pressure to the roller. Roll until the leaves sit flat on the white clay. Remove the paper and put it to one side.

13. Press the alphabet cutter into the surface of the clay, using the flat of your hand to apply even pressure. Move the cutter slightly in both directions to prevent it from sticking to the clay. Lift the cutter out of the outer piece of clay. Gently press the clay left inside the cutter out to one side on the nonstick surface.

14. Turn the clay over onto the white side. Press a magnet into the middle of the clay. Turn it back over and place it on a piece of parchment paper in a foil baking tray.

15. Repeat Steps 13 and 14 with all the letters you have chosen. Preheat the oven to 230°F (110°C). When they are all in the foil tray, cover it with a second tray and heat it in the oven for 30 minutes. When the time is up, remove the tray from the oven and leave the clay to cool entirely before lifting the clay out.

SALT-AND-PEPPER PINCH POT

I've never met a pinch pot I didn't like! They're one of those items you never knew you needed until you make one. They make an incredibly useful storage solution and they look cute. Pinch pots are also satisfying to make. They are named after the process for making them: The clay is pinched into place to create a small vessel. They take about 10 minutes and very little effort to whip up.

The rustic look of this pot is created by sprinkling the clay with ground pepper to give it a soft, food-safe pattern. These small pots are the perfect size for keeping salt and pepper nearby when you're cooking. I like to keep a tray of oils and seasonings I often use next to my stove at all times. It makes life so much easier when you're trying to cook healthy meals from scratch with a toddler in tow.

materials

1.75 oz (50 g) white DAS air-dry clay

1 tbsp (6 g) ground black pepper

Baby oil

Sponge brush or paint brush

Food-safe gloss, such as Decopatch Aquapro

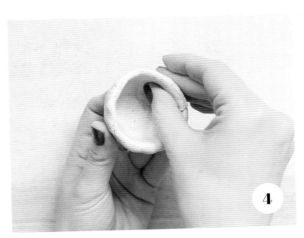

1. Be sure the clay has not dried out and add a sprinkling of water if it looks cracked or firm. With wet hands, roll the clay into a ball. Press the ball flat between your palms, ensuring the clay is smooth and moist.

2. Massage the pepper into the clay. Add a few drops of baby oil to the palms of your hands and rub your hands together, spreading the oil over the surface of your hands.

3. Hold the clay in your hands, sandwiched between your palms. Roll the clay in a circular motion, using very gentle pressure to create a ball.

4. Add a little water to the outside of the ball and smooth the surface. Cup the ball of clay in your hands and push your thumbs into the top of the ball. Place the ball between your thumbs and fingers. Begin to make the hole deeper with your thumbs while at the same time stretching up the remaining clay in the opposite direction with your fingers.

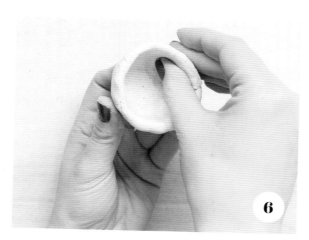

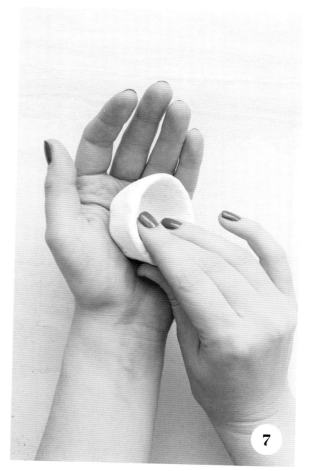

5. The ball should start to look like a pot now.

6. Gently continue to shape the pot in this way, using your thumbs to shape the inside and fingers to shape the outside. You can also hold the pot in the palm of one hand while you shape with the other.

7. Once the pot is even all over, smooth over any cracks with water and your finger.

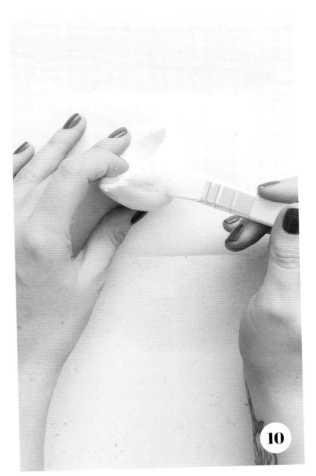

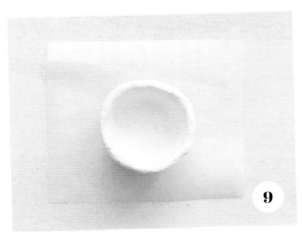

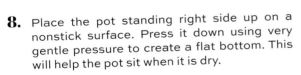

8. Place the pot standing right side up on a nonstick surface. Press it down using very gentle pressure to create a flat bottom. This will help the pot sit when it is dry.

9. Place the pot in a warm, dry area for 48 hours until the clay has dried out and is set.

10. Using a sponge brush, cover the pot in a thin layer of food-safe gloss. Wait for it to dry fully and cover it with a second thin layer of gloss. When this is completely dry, the pot is ready to use.

ABSTRACT FLORAL BLOCK PLATTER

If you're short on space, making kitchen wares useful and chic kills two birds with one stone. I see this platter as a gorgeous way to serve food and as a piece of art in its own right. When you make it yourself, you can create color and texture combinations that are perfect for your space.

We're making a slab for this project, but it's more of a free-form process. The look is abstract and that gives us room for experimenting. This project also channels our creativity to cut freehand shapes. Your shapes will need to be cut from thinly rolled clay; be generous with your parchment paper to help you transfer the shapes to the base of the clay.

materials

1 lb (450 g) white FIMO polymer clay

2 (1 x 15 x 0.25" [2.5 x 38 x 0.6–cm]) lengths of wood

Roller

Ruler

Craft knife

Parchment paper

1.75 oz (50 g) champagne FIMO polymer clay

Toothpick

1.75 oz (50 g) leaf green FIMO polymer clay

1.75 oz (50 g) terra-cotta FIMO polymer clay

1.75 oz (50 g) mustard FIMO polymer clay

1" (2.5-cm) circle cookie cutter

2 (10 x 10" [25 x 25–cm]) foil baking trays

1. Break the white polymer clay into four pieces and warm each one in your hands, rolling and balling up the clay until it is soft and easy to manipulate. When all the clay is soft, bring it back together into a ball.

2. Place the soft clay on a nonstick surface between the lengths of wood. Roll out the clay until the roller runs smoothly over the clay and it's an even thickness with the wood. Measure and cut the clay into a 7 x 10–inch (18 x 25–cm) rectangle.

3. Place the clay on a piece of parchment paper and put it to one side.

4. Take out the next block of clay and hold the clay between your palms to warm it. After 30 seconds, begin to work the clay in your hands. Roll it out, twist it together and ball it back up several times until it is soft and pliable.

5. Place this on a piece of parchment paper. Without using any lengths of wood, roll the clay out thinly.

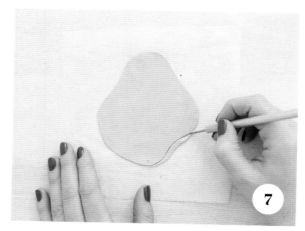

6. Using the toothpick, draw two shapes on the surface of the clay. Get creative!

7. Cut out the shapes with the craft knife. Cut away from your other hand to avoid accidents. It is sometimes easier to cut roughly around the shape, then go back in and cut around more detailed sections later on. When you are finished, remove the clay outside of the shapes.

8. Repeat Steps 4 through 7 with all the colors of clay. I've created different shapes in each color to create a floral element to the pattern.

9. When you have cut shapes from each color clay, lay them on the white block. Build up the pattern, overlapping the shapes in places.

10. Keep building up the pattern over the surface of the clay until you like the final design. Cover the clay with a piece of parchment paper and press it down in between the cutout clay with your fingertips.

11. Place your roller gently on top of the parchment paper and roll along the clay, adding a very small amount of pressure to the roller. Roll until the leaves sit flat on the white clay. Remove the paper and put it to one side.

12. Use the cookie cutter to make a hole in the top of the clay. Press the cookie cutter into the surface of the clay, using the flat of your hand to apply even pressure. Twist the cutter slightly in both directions to prevent it from sticking to the clay. Lift the cutter out of the outer piece of clay. Gently press the circle of clay left inside the cutter out onto a piece of parchment paper.

13. Preheat the oven to 230°F (110°C). Carefully lift the parchment paper, sliding your hand underneath the clay. Transfer the clay and the parchment paper to a foil baking tray and cover it with a second tray. Heat it in the oven for 30 minutes. When the time is up, remove the tray from the oven and leave the clay to cool entirely before lifting the clay out.

HANGING HERB GARDEN PLANTER

Fresh herbs are a game changer when it comes to home cooking. Grow your own! I love having an abundance of fresh herbs when I need them, and at a fraction of the price of buying them.

A hanging planter can save on premium work-surface space in your kitchen and allow you prime positioning in bright sunshine for your herbs. And with this planter you'll never forget which herb is in which pot because we're using clay lettering to label each one.

I'm using smaller fondant alphabet cutters to create the lettering on these pots. Alternatively, you could use a printed template to cut them out with a craft knife.

materials

12 oz (350 g) terra-cotta FIMO polymer clay

2 (1 x 15 x 0.25" [2.5 x 38 x 0.6–cm]) lengths of wood

Roller

3.75" (9.5-cm) circle cookie cutter

2 (1 x 15 x 0.13" [2.5 x 38 x 0.3–cm]) lengths of wood

Ruler

Craft knife

Plastic straw

Flat blending tool

Parchment paper

1 oz (30 g) champagne FIMO polymer clay

Alphabet fondant cutters

2 (10 x 10" [25 x 25–cm]) foil baking trays

Scissors

Cotton cord

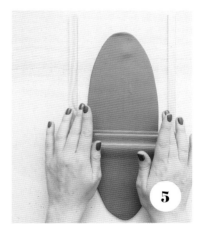

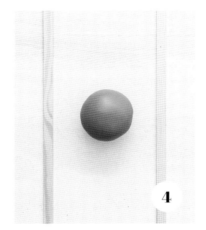

1. Break the clay into four pieces and warm each one in your hands, rolling and balling up the clay until it is soft and easy to manipulate. When all the clay is soft, bring it back together into a ball.

2. Place the soft clay on a nonstick surface between the 0.25-inch (0.6-cm)-thick lengths of wood. Roll out the clay until the roller runs smoothly over the clay and it's an even thickness with the wood.

3. Press the cookie cutter into the surface of the clay, using the flat of your hand to apply even pressure. Twist the cutter slightly in both directions to prevent it from sticking to the clay. Lift the cutter out of the outer piece of clay. Gently press the circle of clay left inside the cutter out to one side on the nonstick surface.

4. Roll the leftover piece back into a ball and place it between the two 0.13-inch (0.3-cm)-thick lengths of wood.

5. Roll out the clay until the roller runs smoothly over both the clay and the wood, creating an even thickness throughout the clay.

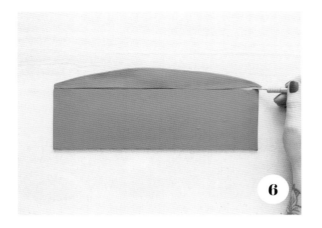

6. Measure and cut a rectangular piece of clay that is 12.5 x 4 inches (32 x 10 cm).

7. Using the straw, make three holes along one long length of the clay. One at 2 inches (5 cm), one at 6 inches (15 cm) and the last 10 inches (25 cm) from the right edge.

8. Wrap the longer edge around the circle piece of clay, making sure the holes in your clay are at the top of the pot and not next to the circle. Carefully line up the long edge with the bottom of the clay circle.

9. Bring the two shorter edges of the rectangle together so they meet along the 0.13-inch (0.3-cm) side. Push them together and gently warm the clay on both sides of the join with your fingers, then use a flat blending tool to blend the clay along the join on both the outside and inside. Place the pot to one side on a piece of parchment paper.

10. Take out the next block of clay and hold the clay between your palms to warm it. After 30 seconds, begin to work the clay in your hands. Roll it out, twist it together and ball it back up several times until it is soft and pliable.

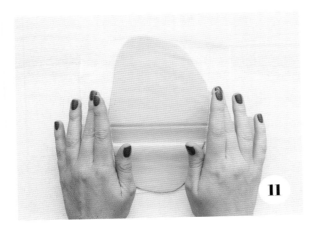

11. Place this on a piece of parchment paper. Without using any lengths of wood, roll the clay out thinly.

12. Press the fondant cutter into the surface of the clay, using the flat of your hand to apply even pressure. Twist the cutter slightly in both directions to prevent it from sticking to the clay. Lift the cutter out of the outer piece of clay. Place the cutter in the freezer for 10 minutes to harden the clay. Gently press the clay left inside the cutter out to one side on the nonstick surface.

13. When you have the letters needed, place them onto the side of the pot. Gently press them down with a blending tool.

14. Preheat the oven to 230°F (110°C). Carefully lift the parchment paper and transfer both the clay and the parchment paper to a foil baking tray. Cover it with a second tray and heat it in the oven for 30 minutes. When the time is up, remove the tray from the oven and leave the clay to cool entirely before lifting the clay out.

15. Tie three 20-inch (50-cm) pieces of cord to the three holes. Bring them together at the other end and tie in a knot.

ACKNOWLEDGMENTS

My first and biggest thank-you has to go to my partner, Alex. Not only have you been my biggest supporter while writing this book, but also during the years in which I've built my business. You have always believed in me, even when I haven't believed in myself. You are my best friend, my champion and the love of my life. I couldn't have done this without you.

My mother, who always encouraged and indulged my creative passions growing up. I will always appreciate the support you've given me more than you know. And my mother-in-law, Pat, a very loving and generous grandma to my beautiful son. We are so very lucky to have you in our lives. This book would not exist if it were not for both of you. Thank you both from the bottom of my heart.

I'd like to thank my editor Rebecca Fofonoff, Meg Baskis and the rest of the team at Page Street Publishing for this opportunity and for bringing my dream project to life. Your encouragement, constructive criticism and gentle suggestions have made me a better writer. A big thank-you to Jenna Nelson Patton for your diligence and patience and for always reassuring me that my mistakes were all part of writing a book.

My last thank-you is a blanket appreciation for all the creative bloggers, influencers and businesswomen who have inspired, enabled and supported me over the past ten years. I would have never made it here without encouragement, a shoulder to lean on and a supportive pep talk every now and then. Even if we've never spoken, I have most likely been inspired by a collective love of creativity and an ambition to build a business and life based around art.

ABOUT THE AUTHOR

Francesca is an award-winning blogger and creative business owner making her home more beautiful with a DIY attitude. She has always believed in combining craft with design to create something that is beautifully handmade, and this ethos is a recurring theme throughout her blog, Fall For DIY. Sharing her ideas and skills with her online following of over half a million is Francesca's passion, and it is the driving force behind her continuously experimenting with techniques both old and new. Francesca's work has been featured in many print and online publications, including *Elle Decoration*, *Design*Sponge*, *Mollie Makes*, *Domino* and Apartment Therapy.

INDEX